Better Homes and Gardens®

Your Baby

COMES HOME

Birth–3 Months

By Edwin Kiester, Jr., and Sally Valente Kiester
and the Editors of Better Homes & Gardens® Books

Photography by
Kathryn Abbe and Frances McLaughlin-Gill

Excerpted from the Better Homes and Gardens® *NEW BABY BOOK*

BETTER HOMES AND GARDENS® BOOKS

Editor: Gerald M. Knox
Art Director: Ernest Shelton
Managing Editor: David A. Kirchner
Editorial Project Managers: James D. Blume, Marsha Jahns,
    Rosanne Weber Mattson, Mary Helen Schiltz

Associate Art Directors: Linda Ford Vermie, Neoma Alt West,
    Randall Yontz
Assistant Art Directors: Lynda Haupert, Harijs Priekulis,
    Tom Wegner
Senior Graphic Designer: Darla Whipple-Frain
Graphic Designers: Mike Burns, Brian Wignall
Art Production: Director, John Berg; Associate, Joe Heuer;
    Office Manager, Emma Rediger

President, Book Group: Fred Stines
Vice President, General Manager: Jeramy Lanigan
Vice President, Retail Marketing: Jamie Martin
Vice President, Administrative Services: Rick Rundall

BETTER HOMES AND GARDENS® MAGAZINE
President, Magazine Group: James A. Autry
Vice President, Editorial Director: Doris Eby
Executive Director, Editorial Services: Duane L. Gregg

MEREDITH CORPORATE OFFICERS
Chairman of the Board: E.T. Meredith III
President: Robert A. Burnett
Executive Vice President: Jack D. Rehm

YOUR BABY COMES HOME
Editorial Project Manager: Mary Helen Schiltz
Graphic Designer: Lynda Haupert
Electronic Text Processor: Paula Forest
Cover Photographer: Bob Ebel

ACKNOWLEDGMENTS

Mary Ward Brady, B.S., R.N., Childbirth Instructor, Marin
    General Hospital, San Rafael, California.
D. Stewart Rowe, M.D., Associate Clinical Professor of
    Pediatrics, University of California, San Francisco.

CONTENTS

A NEW ROUTINE AT HOME

The tiny bundle you bring home from the hospital can shake up your style of living far out of proportion to its modest size. The first three weeks of parenthood have often been called by new parents the longest and most depleting period of adult life. Considering the adjustments that have to be made in your family routine, that may be no exaggeration.

The family circle may be turned topsy-turvy. Sleeping, eating, and working may be governed by when the baby wants to sleep, eat, and socialize. Family relationships, attitudes, and feelings can be knocked off stride. If the baby is your first, the household may crackle with nervousness and anxiety.

Such strain isn't surprising. For perhaps the first time in your life, another human being will be totally dependent on you. You may face a dozen crises a day: Are we feeding enough? Are we feeding too much? Why is the baby crying? Should we pick him or her up? Is a pin sticking the child? Is the baby too warm? Is he or she too cold? Do diapers need changing?

Looking at your robust infant a year from now, you'll laugh at your beginning jitters. Babies thrive despite their parents' inexperience. The main casualties of the first six weeks are mothers' and fathers' nerves. Just relax, follow your instincts, and enjoy the baby. If you're in doubt about some detail of care for your newborn, *ask* for help—and keep asking until you get an answer that satisfies you. That's what doctors, nurses, clinics, more experienced parents, and baby books are for.

THE LARGER FAMILY CIRCLE

Whether or not you get additional help from a friend, relative (your mother or mother-in-law, perhaps), visiting nurse, or housekeeper to assist you during the first few weeks after you return from the hospital is up to you.

Some parents are made even more nervous with another person in the house; they consider a father's help plenty. But an extra pair of hands can be a godsend. First, although mothers aren't invalids, their energy levels may still be below normal. Second, temporarily delegating the household chores to another person gives parents time to get acquainted with the baby and to practice caring for the child.

These first few weeks are important for both parents and infant; don't waste your limited energies doing the family laundry or dusting the furniture while someone else cuddles the baby. Make sure that you have a considerate helper and not a houseguest.

THE OTHER CHILDREN

To you, the arrival of a new baby is a happy event, but an older—and up to now an only—child's feelings may be mixed. Once the sole occupant of the family limelight, he or she now may feel rudely shouldered aside by a demanding newcomer whose every cry brings parents running. No matter how much you reassure the older brother or sister, there's keen competition.

There are no easy answers to what psychologists call sibling rivalry. Preparation helps; before going to the hospital, explain about the baby to the other children, and try to emphasize that the arrival of the newcomer will not lessen your love for them. For children old enough to read, books about the arrival of a new baby are available. Buy younger children a doll to feed and diaper. And if the new baby was born at home or in the presence of the family in an alternative birth center, perhaps the lesson already has been reinforced. Yet the feeling of jealousy is a natural one for a small child, and the actual event may evoke some strong reactions.

A three-year-old may now insist on being treated like a baby—and behave like one. He or she may demand the bottle that had been given up months before. It's not uncommon for children long since past such stages to begin wetting their pants or sucking their thumbs again.

Fortunately, children adjust. You can't ignore their feelings, but don't chide or punish them. All you can do to ease the situation is assure them of your love for them, spend as much time as you can exclusively with them, and try to include them in caring for the new baby. A small gift for the older child may help when someone brings a gift for the baby. If the other child is under three, a word of caution: he or she should never be left alone with the baby.

THE SHARING OF PARENTHOOD

Most fathers today expect to take a full role in child care, and, according to one survey, in about one-fourth of homes, the father, rather than the mother, will be the primary care provider. About half the enrollment in hospital baby-care classes is male. This division of responsibilities means that in many homes decisions about child care are mutually arrived at.

Still, this "new" parenthood doesn't apply to every household. Many men have never had the opportunity to change diapers or bathe an infant. Even today, some grown men have never held a baby in their arms. Part of the new mother's role may be to impart her own, possibly limited, knowledge to her spouse. The first few weeks may be a time of learning together.

Meanwhile, don't forget you are partners as well as parents. The stress of parenthood strains your relationship, too, as each of you may concentrate on the baby and neglect the other. Fathers often feel jealous of the little being who may monopolize the mother's time, while mothers seethe at the paternal pride that focuses on the offspring as it downplays her contribution.

These feelings are normal, and they can be overcome. As soon as you can possibly do so, spend some time with each other. Leave the baby with someone you can trust, and go out for the evening—even if it's only to the nearest fast-food spot.

Fathers today often take an equal—or even primary—role in child care with mothers. In an increasing number of households, it's the man who stays home with the children during the day.

BABY SETS A SCHEDULE

The first few days and nights with the baby will pass in one big blur, as one feeding blends fuzzily into the next. But soon you'll see that the baby's life (and therefore yours) falls into a regular routine.

In more dogmatic days, infants were fed every four hours, whether they were hungry or not. Now most doctors recommend a more flexible schedule. Babies eat when they announce they're hungry.

Baby's whims, unfortunately, aren't always convenient for you. Observe the baby's own pattern of eating and sleeping for a few days, and then construct your schedule accordingly.

Usually, a newborn will want to be fed six to eight times a day, about two to five hours apart. If you feed the baby at 6 a.m., you may expect to do so again at roughly 10 a.m., 2 p.m., 6 p.m., 10 p.m., and 2 a.m.

But few babies are that regular. A baby may be fed at 6 a.m., ask for more at 9 a.m., then go without eating until 2 p.m. On the average, a breast-fed baby requires more frequent feedings than a bottle-fed infant; eight feedings daily at intervals of two to three hours is typical, and some even wish to be fed every hour. But appetite is as individual in babies as in adults. Your bottle-feeder may feed just as frequently or infrequently as the breast-feeder next door. And some babies simply seem to be hungry all the time, eating regularly every three hours around the clock. All these patterns are normal.

As for sleeping, a newborn averages 16 hours a day and may be drowsy or half-awake several additional hours. However, some babies sleep as little as eight hours and yet are not at all deprived of sleep.

Eventually, one nap lengthens and the number of feedings falls to five a day. This usually occurs at about five weeks or when the baby's weight reaches 11 pounds. With luck, the longer nap comes at night, and the periods when the baby is alert come during the day, when you can enjoy them.

Once you understand the baby's schedule, sometimes you can influence it. If the baby seems to sleep through a daytime feeding, wake and feed on schedule; he or she *may* take a longer nap. If the baby dozes during a feeding or falls asleep before it is finished, nudge the child so that he or she does not wake up again in two hours for refueling.

You may want to schedule the baby's bath in the morning, after the early feeding, then put the newborn to bed until another feeding is necessary. Afternoon is a good time for an airing or a stroll, when the sun is higher and the air warmer. By letting the baby catnap during the day, you may be able to keep the child awake at dinner time to socialize with the family.

Remember that the baby's welfare is important, but it can't completely dominate the family's life. When it's time for a nap, put the baby in a crib or bassinet in his or her own room, close the door, and go about your business. Do not tiptoe or caution the other children to "Hush!" Artificial silence only conditions the newcomer to wake at the slightest noise.

YOUR OWN RECOVERY

Legend says pioneer women gave birth in the morning and plowed the back 40 in the afternoon. If so, they must have been exhausted by evening. Bearing and caring for a baby are fatiguing activities.

During these early weeks, take advantage of every opportunity to rest, preferably with your feet up. Keep strenuous work to a minimum; don't set out to do the spring cleaning. Take naps when you can, because it may be difficult to get eight hours of uninterrupted sleep at night. Family finances and the strictures of your maternity leave may dictate when you return to work outside the home, of course, but a customary minimum is six weeks.

The exercises on pages 34 and 35 will help restore your figure by tightening the abdominal muscles that stretched to accommodate the expanded uterus. Physical activity also will help trim any excessive poundage you may have accumulated during pregnancy. A girdle helps support the abdomen. If you're breast-feeding, wear a supporting brassiere during the day and while you're sleeping.

Watch your diet carefully. Breast-feeding requires that you eat for two, but if you limit junk foods and unnecessary calories, your figure won't suffer. If you're not breast-feeding, limit the food you eat. You may have eaten larger meals during pregnancy; now try fewer than 2,000 calories daily. Proper eating and exercise can restore your figure to normal within three months.

WHEN THE BABY CRIES

Babies have only one way to communicate at first: they cry. Your job is to interpret your baby's cries and decide how to respond, if at all.

In time, translation will become second nature. You'll learn to distinguish the tired cry, the hungry cry, the I'm-lonely-someone-come-and-pay-attention-to-me cry. But at first all cries may sound alike: what *is* that child crying about?

Usually, a child cries because another feeding is in order. If the clock shows the baby hasn't eaten in three or four hours, you almost can be sure the message is "Come feed me."

When babies continue to cry after eating, it may mean they're not getting enough to eat. If you're breast-feeding, allow time for a longer feeding, or offer a supplementary bottle. If the baby is bottle-fed, increase the amount.

Sometimes the cause of crying is obvious. It may be something as simple as a soiled diaper or the discomfort of diaper rash (see page 24). A few babies cry at sudden change, or are startled by a loud noise. Some cry when they are too warm or too cold.

Older babies may cry because they're lonely. The infant, wanting to see faces and hear voices, may call for a visitor.

The cry seldom signals a real emergency. Despite parents' fears, an open diaper pin is seldom the cause. A medical explanation is equally rare and is usually indicated by other signs, such as fever, decreased appetite, nasal congestion, vomiting, and diarrhea. Thus you seldom need to drop what you're doing and respond to the baby's cries. But don't let crying continue for more than a few minutes without investigation.

THE CRYING HOUR

Some babies cry persistently without explanation. In fact, about one-fourth of the parents who visit well-baby clinics report their infants fall into this category. The crying is harmless for the baby, but nerve-wracking and exhausting for parents, particularly when they seek an explanation and cannot find one. The problem seems to be most persistent around six weeks. It may stop shortly thereafter, and seldom lasts more than three months.

For many of these babies, a daily "crying hour" develops, mostly in late afternoon, but sometimes in the morning or late at night. The baby often reddens, draws knees up to chest, and kicks and screams loudly. As each cry subsides, another begins. The length of the "crying hour" varies. Some normal infants cry six to seven hours a day.

This regular, persistent crying is sometimes called "colic," because it was previously believed to result from intestinal cramping. Most doctors now doubt this explanation. It is based on the observation that "colicky" babies draw up their legs, distend their abdomens, and pass gas. But babies do this at other times, too.

Intolerance of formula is sometimes blamed for colic, but changing the ingredients seldom lessens crying. (And breast-fed babies cry, too.) Other theorists, noting that the crying hour often coincides with late afternoon when parents are likely to be most frazzled, attribute the baby's crying to family emotional stress. Emotional stress may indeed exist when babies cry for hours on end, but it is difficult to determine which came first, crying or stress. Moreover, babies of experienced, calm parents are not immune from crying.

The most logical (and comforting) explanation for persistent crying is a developmental one. Babies cry because their nervous systems are still maturing. The regular daily pattern and the fact that the baby seems to "grow out of it" by the age of three months, no matter what steps are taken, supports this point. It is further substantiated by folklore parents have known for centuries that soothing, rhythmic sounds and motions have a calming effect on a crying baby.

To soothe a crying baby, the first step is an age-old one. Try rocking to and fro in a rhythmic, tick-tock way. Holding the baby in an upright or semisitting position seems to work better than cradling him or her in a horizontal posture. Other rhythmic motions in a sitting position may help. Some parents find that a car or bus ride—even a short one—will halt the crying. At home, try a mechanical wind-up swing, which will keep the baby rocking for 10 to 15 minutes.

The rhythm of music and sound helps, too. You sing to the baby—that's where lullabies originated—or play the radio or stereo. Even the regular, continuous noise of a vacuum sweeper or vaporizer may be soothing.

However, no harm is done if you simply let the baby cry until he or she stops, as he or she eventually will. Persistent crying does no physical damage. That presupposes that you can tolerate it, and that it does not disturb the neighbors.

The "crying hour" can be a great strain for parents. It is normal and natural to feel frustrated and angry at a tiny child who continues to shriek hour after hour despite your most solicitous efforts. It is particularly difficult for a parent who is left alone with the child and calls for plenty of mutual support.

THE BABY IS HUNGRY

Whether you feed by breast or bottle, baby's meals will consume time. At an average of 30 minutes per session, you'll devote three full hours to six or more daily feedings.

You won't have difficulty recognizing when it's time for a feeding. Even before the baby is fully awake, you'll hear fussing—a restless moving in the crib. Next will come a sucking, slurping noise as the baby tries to get fists into mouth and, succeeding, gnaws on them. Then there'll be a tentative cry or two, the cries coming closer together until—if you wait long enough—a series of lusty squalls will send the message in no uncertain terms.

Even if you're fast asleep, your subconscious will pick up the baby's signal. In fact, some nursing mothers say the baby's first cries unconsciously start the milk let-down reflex.

Round-the-clock feedings usually continue for approximately one to three months. Then the baby may begin to sleep through one of the feedings, lengthening that particular nap to six or more hours. Your baby may be erratic for a time, missing a feeding, then reverting to the old schedule for a night or two, then missing it again. You may try to induce a longer sleep by providing an extra large feeding in the evening or by waking the baby for feedings during the day, so the rest at night is a longer one.

BREAST-FEEDING AT HOME

It may not be so easy to breast-feed at home as it was in the hospital. You'll be faced by interruptions and conflicts when the baby's demands interfere with your other obligations. Many a nursing mother feels overwhelmed and gives up the project. One doctor recalls a mother whose milk dried up when she was welcomed home by a week's accumulation of dirty laundry!

For your part, this period calls for perseverance. It's a difficult time, for the baby's appetite may vary widely, leading you to feel inadequate and uncertain about your milk supply. And being solely responsible for the baby's feeding can make you feel terribly tied down. It's important to overcome these feelings and recognize that you really needn't restrict yourself.

If breast-feeding is to succeed, your family must help, too. Your milk supply will be enhanced if you are rested and relaxed, rather than fatigued and tense. Rest is essential. So is assistance with household chores. If you haven't hired someone to help and no relatives are available, the father and any other children must pitch in, or some tasks must be postponed for a few weeks.

THE NURSING MOTHER'S DIET

As the baby's sole source of nourishment, you must eat well yourself. As a general rule, a nursing mother needs about 300 calories more than when she was pregnant and 600 more than before pregnancy. She requires an even greater number if she is under 20 and still growing herself. Of course, telling you to eat more may be gratuitous advice. You'll probably find, perhaps to your dismay, that you have a ravenous appetite.

A well-balanced diet is essential, including daily servings from each of the basic food groups of protein foods, milk and milk products, grains, and fruits and vegetables. The diet differs slightly from the one you followed during pregnancy. You need less protein and more vitamin-rich foods. The doctor may prescribe that you continue your iron supplement and multiple vitamins. The baby also may be given supplementary vitamin D.

You also need a good supply of calcium. The easiest way to get it is via a daily quart of milk, which supplies this important mineral for the baby's bones and teeth as well as providing a liquid base for the milk supply and your digestive wastes. You should take in plenty of other fluids daily. Drink a glass of water before and after each feeding.

If you're concerned about your weight, substitute low-fat or fat-free milk. Or your doctor may suggest calcium tablets. You also may use milk in puddings, custards, or soups. Other liquids may be coffee, tea, juices, or broth. Avoid carbonated drinks.

Just about anything you eat or drink may find its way into your milk supply. The flavor of onions and garlic comes through almost unchanged. Some babies will refuse to nurse if the taste is particularly strong. If you eat chocolate, it is said the baby will have diarrhea, although the relationship never has been definitely established. A meal of beans or cabbage is said to cause indigestion in the baby.

Be sparing with drugs, cigarettes, and alcohol. Aspirin or mild laxatives probably are not harmful, although you may want to ask your doctor before using them. Barbiturates, tranquilizers, and other stronger medications should be taken only for good medical reasons. Some doctors oppose the use of oral contraceptives by nursing mothers.

The potential harm of cigarette smoking by nursing mothers still is being investigated. To be on the safe side, don't smoke. Some doctors

approve an occasional glass of wine to relax after a tense day and stimulate the mother's let-down reflex. But they caution that too much alcohol can make the baby woozy after breast-feeding.

You may be tempted to reduce your weight during this period, but it is not a time for strict dieting. Both you and the baby may suffer. During nursing, priority goes to building up the breast milk.

The following is a sample menu to be used during nursing:

Breakfast
Small glass orange juice
½ cup oatmeal with brown sugar
Full cup milk (some may be used on oatmeal)
Coffee or tea

Lunch
Tuna fish sandwich made with 2 slices of whole wheat bread, ½ cup tuna fish salad
1 small banana
Full cup milk

Afternoon snack
½ cup peanuts
Full cup milk

Dinner
Six ounces of roast beef
½ cup egg noodles
¾ cup cut asparagus
Spinach salad with oil and vinegar
Full cup milk
Coffee or tea

Evening snack
2 oatmeal-raisin cookies
Full cup milk

BREAST-FEEDING AND VISITORS

You may not want many visitors during the first few weeks you are breast-feeding. Company and excitement can hold back the milk flow and result in a less than satisfactory feeding. Guests shouldn't be allowed to interfere with the nursing schedule. For your own comfort, don't delay the feeding more than a few minutes.

Some mothers are embarrassed to nurse before other people—or feel their guests might be embarrassed. Writers who discuss etiquette divide on whether public display of this natural function is socially acceptable. But like many aspects of motherhood, the question doesn't involve protocol—just follow your own judgment. Nursing is natural and nothing to be ashamed of. Indeed, many offices provide places where employees may nurse their babies.

Regardless of your feelings, be sure to explain nursing to your other children. Make it clear that nursing is a perfectly natural phenomenon, a warm human experience between mothers and babies to be shared by the members of the entire family. In fact, it can be an early lesson in sexual difference for the older children, showing that mothers nurse babies and fathers don't.

Once you've established a regular nursing routine and feel more relaxed about it, you'll probably find no need to be isolated from the rest of the family; nursing can be a time to enjoy the other children. It provides the opportunity for conversation, for playing games with the other children, or for story-telling.

A TIME AND PLACE

With experience, you'll be able to nurse the baby anywhere. Some mothers say they can nurse while standing or walking. But your early nursing will be more successful if you establish a relaxed, regular routine. A quiet room is best. Pick a chair with arms, bolster your elbows with pillows, and prop your feet up. Use the time exclusively to cuddle and talk to the baby, not watch television or read. At night, take the baby into bed with you, so you can rest while nursing.

For your own comfort and the baby's, nurse when the baby is ready to eat. He or she will probably follow a three-hour schedule, but if the baby wakes early, don't wait for the three hours to pass. On the other hand, if the baby oversleeps, rouse the child and begin feeding. Otherwise, your breasts may feel full and sore; and milk may begin to leak on your clothing.

Once a routine is established, you'll probably nurse about ten minutes on each breast. More than that is probably fruitless. Even slow eaters get about four-fifths of their capacity in the first five minutes. Some babies are satisfied with just one breast. Remember that suckling itself is important; the baby may be kept at the breast a few minutes to satisfy this instinct. But prolonged sucking can cause sore nipples. You may wish to substitute a pacifier.

WILL YOU HAVE ENOUGH MILK?

Only rarely does a woman have too little milk for her baby. The human breast normally manufactures one and one-half to two ounces of milk in each breast every three hours. A newborn requires only about two fluid ounces per pound of body weight a day. A seven-pounder thus needs 14 to 21 ounces a day, compared to a normal output of 24 to 32 ounces.

The milk will be rich enough, too. A seven-pound baby needs about 50 calories per pound of body weight per day—350 calories daily. Breast milk measures about 20 calories per ounce, so that amounts to approximately 80 calories per feeding.

Some nursing mothers become discouraged when they first see breast milk. It just doesn't look very nourishing. It's not foamy and white, like milk you pour from a bottle, but resembles skim milk—thin, watery, and slightly blue. But that color and consistency is just right for the baby's development.

A true gauge of your milk's quality and amount is how well the baby grows. If he or she seems to be thriving and filling out, you're furnishing an ample amount of nutrition. Most babies lose a little when they first leave the hospital, but then begin to gain at the rate of about a quarter of a pound per week—noticeable even to an unpracticed eye. In any case, the doctor will weigh the baby at the first checkup.

Another yardstick is how many diapers are used. More than six wet diapers a day usually indicates the baby is getting plenty of fluid.

Don't automatically assume that if your baby won't eat, there's something wrong with your milk. Bottle-fed babies also fuss, cry, spit up, or refuse to eat sometimes.

BREAST-FEEDING AND HEALTH

"Human milk is for the human infant; cow's milk is for the calf." With those words, the late nutritionist Dr. Paul Gyorgy once summed up the pro-breast-feeding side of the continuing controversy over the comparative value of breast milk and its most common substitute.

Even the commercial manufacturers of formula acknowledge that breast milk is the most appropriate nourishment for newborns. And despite conscientious efforts, manufacturers never have been able to duplicate breast milk, although their products contain all essential nutrients.

But are breast-fed babies healthier? They certainly are in less developed countries, where hygiene, water purity, and refrigeration aren't up to Western standards. In the U.S. the picture is less clear, with some studies seeming to show fewer health problems among the breast-fed, and others showing no difference in the health of breast- vs. formula-fed babies when such variables as economic status are considered.

The La Leche League International, the organization that has done most to foster the return of breast-feeding in the U.S., firmly advocates breast-feeding for infant health reasons and cites these purported advantages:

• **Fewer infections.** Breast-fed babies appear to have fewer intestinal infections and fewer respiratory infections, according to research conducted by several investigators. There also is said to be less diarrhea, spitting up, and constipation. Breast-feeding seems to protect against enterocolitis, a condition that is common among bottle-fed babies. Natural immunity to polio, measles, mumps, and other viral infections appears to be prolonged among the breast-fed.

• **Fewer allergies.** Eczema and other common skin rashes of infancy are less frequent among breast-fed babies, the La Leche League states on the basis of several research studies. The breast-fed babies also have fewer allergic sensitivities in later childhood and adulthood. Of course, those babies who are breast-fed exclusively also are free of infancy's most common allergy, a sensitivity to cow's milk.

• **More consistent growth.** Human milk is utilized more quickly by the body, one reason breast-fed babies are fed more frequently than bottle-fed babies. Breast milk also provides the exact nutrients, in the proper quantities, that the baby needs for growth. Because breast milk is digested easily, it can be used immediately.

Other doctors question these conclusions, saying that carefully designed studies have failed to support them.

The American Academy of Pediatrics (AAP), however, has suggested that bottle-fed babies may have more problems with obesity later—a concern in overweight America. The AAP statement said that formula-feeding parents may push babies to consume the full amount offered, which can pile up unnecessary ingredients the body cannot use immediately, and lead to poor eating habits in adulthood.

IT'S NOT JUST MILK

When it was first reported that breast-fed babies had fewer infections, it was thought they were healthier because their supply of food was protected against contamination. More recent investigation shows that breast milk transfers disease-fighting antibodies from mother to child, including white blood cells that combat infection.

The flow of antibodies begins even before the milk itself arrives. Colostrum, the yellowish fluid that comes from the breast before delivery and continues after the baby is born, is a chief source of immunizing substances. It also contains a substance that has a mild laxative effect on the baby, to clear the young digestive system of meconium, the fetal waste. And it has the proper proportion of proteins and fats for the baby's early feedings.

PSYCHOLOGICAL BENEFITS

Nursing sometimes is called the very essence of mothering, and the benefits to both mother and child may go well beyond merely providing nutrition.

At the mother's breast, a baby not only satisfies the need for food, but apparently the equally universal need for warmth, security, and love. In a subtle way, the rhythm of the mother's movements introduces the baby to the rhythm of life. For the mother, breast-feeding fulfills her own need to nurture and love. The two-way exchange of gratification helps to cement the bond between mother and child that continues for a lifetime.

The bond formed in breast-feeding is not something unique to American women and their infants. It extends across a wide spectrum of primitive and sophisticated societies, according to Dr. Derrick Jelliffe, of the University of Southern California School of Medicine, who has studied nursing practices in cultures and countries throughout the world. For both mother and child, Dr. Jelliffe says, breast-feeding seems to satisfy a universal emotional need.

Of course, there are more prosaic advantages to breast-feeding: it's inexpensive, it's convenient, and it's easy. You don't have to prepare formula, sterilize bottles, or clean up afterward. The supply is always on hand in the right amounts and at the right temperatures. When you travel, you don't have to pack anything—the supply travels with you. And the La Leche League estimates that you could hire cleaning help for six months with the money you save on commercial formula and baby food!

CAN ANYONE BREAST-FEED?

The size of a woman's breasts has nothing to do with the ability to nourish her child. Milk production is determined by a network of vessels and canals within the breast. The woman who wears a small bra has just as extensive a network as does her more amply endowed neighbor. Also, for nipples that are flat or are turned inward, patience and special care—augmented by some relatively simple exercises—usually can overcome these difficulties.

WORKING AND BREAST-FEEDING

One reason you may decide not to breast-feed, or may discontinue the practice early, is a desire to return to your career. According to the La Leche League, it's possible, however, to continue breast-feeding while working, and a rapidly growing number of mothers are doing so.

How this works for you will depend upon the convenience for you and baby to be united during the working day. Some women are able to breast-feed right at work, either because the employer operates an affiliated child-care center or because the person caring for the child brings him or her to the mother at feeding time. If you're working near your home, of course, you may simply return there during your lunch period.

Even if you can't be with the baby at feeding time, you can continue to provide breast milk by hand-expressing into a relief bottle that then can be given to the child by another person. Many women perform hand-expression during working hours, so that breast milk continues to be produced on schedule. The milk is then refrigerated or kept in a chilled vacuum bottle.

Women who plan to breast-feed usually do not resume their jobs until the baby is at least six to ten weeks old, by which time he or she may have reduced the number of feedings, and others wait until four to six months, when the child may obtain some nourishment from solid foods. But some women hold jobs and continue to breast-feed the child exclusively until one year or older.

THE HUSBAND'S ROLE IN FEEDING

If your baby is formula-fed, father automatically takes part. Mother and father can alternate feedings, depending on who's available. The baby isn't likely to complain.

Breast-feeding, of course, is different. But a hand-expressed relief bottle allows the father to feed the baby, especially if you're planning to go out alone, or if the father cares for the child during the day. For nighttime feeding, it can be the father's responsibility to get up and bring the child to you. Another role for the father, breast-feeding advocates say, is to provide moral support and companionship, and to encourage you to continue with this natural form of nutrition. The father also can take over a larger share of the household duties and spend more time with the other children. That leaves you free for nursing and for the routine of baby care.

For formula-feeding, take a prepared bottle from refrigerator, shake, and warm under hot-water faucet.

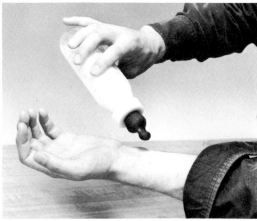

Test temperature by sprinkling a few drops on inside of wrist. It should feel warm, not hot.

Prop the baby in semi-sitting position in crook of elbow, for easier breathing and swallowing.

SUPPLEMENTARY AND RELIEF BOTTLES

If your baby still seems unsatisfied and continues to cry after being placed at the second breast, your doctor may suggest you offer a supplementary bottle immediately afterward. Regularly supplementing breast milk with formula is usually a last resort, however. As part of the supply-demand principle, your milk production will drop. And the baby may later resist the more difficult task of breast-feeding. Giving water isn't necessary except in hot weather.

After a few days, you may wish to provide a relief bottle, so the baby becomes accustomed to bottle-feeding and you can get an occasional respite. That's also a way to bring the father into the feeding routine and allow him a private period with the baby. Your own milk is the best supply. Hand-express milk from your breast, or use a breast pump to squeeze it from the nipple into a sterile bottle. Refrigerate until needed. This way you'll maintain your milk production.

When the baby is down to four or five feedings per day, relief bottles may be used more often. By then, the baby has become accomplished at nursing and may readily switch between breast and bottle; you will now be freer to leave him or her and resume working outside the home. When you are absent from home at feeding time, you always should nurse as soon as you return, so you can relieve the fullness in your breasts and continue to produce milk. Especially in the early weeks, some milk may leak from your breasts and retard the flow. If it occurs regularly, you may wish to wear a folded handkerchief inside your nursing bra.

BOTTLE-FEEDING

The majority of babies are bottle-fed, including many who started on breast milk. Babies brought up on formula thrive, too, so don't hesitate to feed yours by bottle or to switch from breast milk to formula if you find nursing unsatisfactory. The choice of feeding method is an individual matter.

On the average, bottle-fed newborns eat about six times a day, once every four hours. A newborn takes about two ounces at each feeding. The amount increases as the baby grows older, and the number of feedings decreases.

As with breast-feeding, bottle-feeding comes naturally. Because you'll be there for 30 minutes or more, pick a comfortable armchair or the corner of a sofa, with pillows to support your elbows. Hold the baby in your lap, the head in the crook of one elbow, the bottle in your other hand. The baby should be in a semisitting position, to keep the airway open and allow easy swallowing. Don't feed while the baby is lying on his or her back; gagging may result.

When you tickle the cheek or lips, the baby instinctively will turn, seize the nipple, and begin to suck. Hold the bottle at slightly more than a right angle to the baby's mouth, so the nipple and cap are filled with formula and not air, which causes a false fullness and makes the baby uncomfortable.

Keep the cap of the bottle slightly loose to allow air to enter. A line of bubbles will rise through the formula to indicate the baby is feeding successfully. Place a folded diaper or bib under the chin to catch dribbles.

Sometimes the baby may pull so hard that a kind of negative pressure builds up in the bottle. The nipple or plastic bottle liner collapses and shuts off the flow. The frustrated baby continues to suck but gets nothing for the effort. To prevent this, move the bottle in the baby's mouth from time to time to break the suction, or remove it entirely for a moment.

Your baby may not finish the entire bottle at each feeding. Just like adults, babies have the right not to be hungry sometimes. Don't coax him or her to finish.

On the other hand, if the baby repeatedly devours the bottle's contents and seems to want more, increase the next feeding by one-half ounce. When that amount no longer satisfies the baby, add another half-ounce. Try to keep just a little ahead in matching supply to demand.

Don't prop the bottle and leave. That practice not only denies the baby some necessary parenting, it can be dangerous. If the milk flows too quickly, it may cause the baby to gag or vomit, then choke by sucking matter into the lungs. And if the bottle slips away and the baby can't recover it, the experience can be downright frustrating.

PREPARING THE FORMULA

You can mix cow's milk or evaporated milk with other ingredients to make an acceptable substitute for mother's milk, but few parents follow this complicated procedure today. More commonly, they use commercial, premixed formulas, which are more nourishing and more convenient and save time.

Sold under various brand names in supermarkets and drugstores, the formulas come in three types:

• Powdered formula is mixed with warm water, a scoop of formula per two ounces of water. It is the least expensive variety.

• Liquid concentrate also must be mixed, usually one part of concentrate to one of water. It is available in 13-ounce cans and must be refrigerated after opening.

• Ready-to-feed formula may be used directly from the can, requiring no mixing. It is the most expensive kind. Disposable bottles, the ultimate convenience, require only a nipple to be used for immediate feeding.

Commercial formulas are said to contain the important ingredients of mother's milk in the correct proportions, and manufacturers improve them as knowledge is gained. Most use cow's milk as the basic source of protein. Others use vegetable protein, usually from soybeans, and may be recommended for babies with allergies or for babies born into families with allergic reactions to milk. The American Academy of Pediatrics recommends that formula fortified with iron be used by the age of four months.

Preparing formula isn't such a big deal, as it used to be when sanitation and sterilization methods were less sure than they are today. With improved hygiene, a relatively pure water supply, and presterilized formula, the elaborate sterilization measures are considered unnecessary by many doctors and parents, except in unusual cases. Instead, you simply prepare the formula as you need it, one bottle at a time.

If you own a dishwasher, rinse out the bottles after use and wash and dry them in the washer's bottom rack. Wash the nipples in the dishwasher, too, or sterilize them separately in a pot of boiling water, storing them in a jar until ready for use. If you use ready-to-feed formula, pour the prescribed amount into a bottle, cover with a nipple, and feed. Liquid concentrate or powder can be mixed with warm water directly from the faucet. Just add the right amount of liquid or powdered formula, cap with the nipple, shake the bottle, and feed.

If you don't have a dishwasher or aren't certain about your water supply, you may wish to follow another method. Wash and rinse the used bottles, nipples, rings, and caps by hand, then fill each bottle with the prescribed amount of water. Cover with nipples and caps, and boil in a sterilizer for 25 minutes. After the bottles have cooled, remove them from the sterilizer, and store them at room temperature until needed. Then add formula, cap, shake, and use without heating. An advantage to this method is that you open formula only as necessary.

You may also sterilize one bottle at a time. Wash and rinse the bottle and nipple after use, then place them in an uncovered saucepan of water; boil for five minutes. Remove with tongs, pour in the prescribed amount of water from the saucepan in which the materials were sterilized, add formula, shake, and use.

TERMINAL STERILIZATION

The traditional method of preparing formula is called the terminal method, which enables you to prepare a day's supply of formula at a time. It is still favored by many parents and pediatricians.

To prepare formula this way, you should have a set place in the kitchen, near stove, sink, and refrigerator. It should be equipped with the following, which may be bought as a kit:

• Eight eight-ounce glass or plastic bottles, with nipples, screw-on rings, and covers.
• Two or three four-ounce bottles for water.
• A quart measuring pitcher that is graduated in ounces.
• Punch can opener.
• Bottle and nipple brushes.
• Long-handle spoon for stirring.
• Funnel and tongs.
• Jar with lid for storing extra nipples.
• A sterilizer or a large pot with a tight lid.

It must be deep enough so the bottles are kept off the bottom and nipples don't touch the lid.
• A rack for the sterilizer, to keep the bottles away from the bottom of the kettle.

After a bottle has been used, rinse the formula from it with clean water. Remove and rinse the nipples, squeezing water through them to remove scum or butterfat from the holes. When ready to prepare formula, wash bottles, nipples, caps, and nipple covers in hot, sudsy water, using a detergent, which cuts scum better than soap does. Use a bottle brush to clean the insides of the bottles, and a nipple brush to cleanse scum or dried formula from the nipples. Also wash the measuring pitcher, can opener, tongs, and the other utensils, rinsing everything in hot, clean water.

With soap, wash the top of the can containing liquid formula and wash well.

Next, follow these steps:

1. Measure the prescribed number of ounces of warm water into the graduated pitcher.

2. Add a full can of concentrated formula, or specified amount of powdered formula, and stir with the long-handle spoon. Always add concentrated or powdered formula *to* the water.

3. Pour the mixture into the clean bottles— about one more ounce per bottle than you expect the baby to drink.

4. Put nipples, rings, and caps on bottles, leaving rings loose so steam can escape.

5. Place the bottles on the sterilizer rack or kettle. Add about three inches of water.

6. Bring the water to a boil, cover, reduce heat, and allow it to boil gently for 25 minutes.

7. Remove sterilizer from heat, and allow to cool until you can touch it.

8. Remove the lid and cool the bottles gradually by adding cool water. (Gradual cooling keeps scum from forming.)

9. Remove bottles and tighten caps.

10. Store in refrigerator until ready to use.

11. Before feeding, warm the bottle by heating it in a small saucepan of water, by placing it under the hot water faucet for a few minutes, or by using a bottle warmer. Shake a few drops on your wrist to test the temperature. It should feel pleasantly warm, not too hot or cold.

BOTTLE PREPARATION METHODS

DISPOSABLE BOTTLES

To prepare formula with disposable bottles, sterilize nipples, rings, and caps by boiling five minutes in pan.

Nipples, rings, and caps also may be sterilized in dishwasher. Place in covered basket on top rack.

Remove single formula sac from roll, tearing at perforation. Don't touch the inside of the sac.

Slide the disposable bottle liner into holder by folding lengthwise. Hold liner by tabs only.

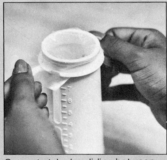

Separate tabs by sliding between fingers; pull over rim at top of holder. Tear off tabs; dispose.

Fill with formula; snap on nipple and cap. Or use sterilized water; add formula when ready to use.

SIMPLE METHOD

Simple method of preparing bottles kills bacteria with hot water from the dishwasher.

Sterilize nipples in saucepan or dishwasher, then store in a jar until ready for use.

Fill with correct amount of tap water, cap with nipple, then add formula at feeding time.

Prepare a bottle of formula as you need it or a day's supply at one time. Formula and equipment are usually sterilized to kill harmful bacteria; the most popular methods are shown here. Prepared formula always should be stored in the refrigerator.

TERMINAL METHOD

Terminal method is traditional way to sterilize. First, wash bottles and nipples in sudsy water.

Drain bottles on cloth or paper towel; be sure to clean all caked milk from nipple openings.

Clean top of formula can with boiling water; use a sterilized punch opener to open the can.

Measure the prescribed amount of warm water from the tap into a graduated pitcher that holds one quart of liquid.

To the water, add the concentrated formula or powder according to the directions, and stir with a long-handled spoon.

Pour the proper amount of liquid into each bottle. Be sure to use a funnel to prevent spilling the mixture.

Put nipples, rings, and caps on bottles. Make sure the rings remain loose so steam can escape from the bottles.

To sterilize the bottles, place them on a rack in the sterilizer. Add three inches of water. Boil gently for 25 minutes.

Remove the bottles from heat, and allow them to cool gradually for about two hours. Tighten caps. Store in refrigerator.

STORING FORMULA

Bacteria grow rapidly in milk. Don't give the baby an unfinished bottle of formula unless he or she is definitely hungry again within an hour.

Be sure to refrigerate the formula as soon as it has cooled after sterilization. It will then keep as long as ordinary milk. Canned formula must always be refrigerated after opening; cover the top with aluminum foil or plastic wrap. You might mark it with date and time.

DISPOSABLE BOTTLES

Disposable bottles are a definite convenience in busy households, and some doctors insist that babies fed with them are healthier, perhaps happier, and have less colic, too, although this has not been established scientifically.

Disposable bottles are narrow sacs of transparent plastic, bought in a roll, torn off for individual use, and thrown away afterward. A complete bottle preparation kit usually includes a roll of sacs, unbreakable plastic sac holders, nipples, retaining rings, and covers. If you've inherited an older kit, you may find a metal expander that was used before the advent of the plastic tabs that are now present on most disposable bottles.

Prepare either a day's supply or a bottle at a time. Wash and dry the retaining rings, nipples, and nipple covers in your dishwasher. You can buy a nipple holder that will fit the top rack. Let nipples and rings dry until cool.

When they've cooled, tear one sac from the roll at the perforation and fold it lengthwise. Grasp it at the tabs and insert the sac in the bottle holder. Next, pull the tabs apart and slide them over the top of the holder. Pull down on the tabs (with an even motion) until they cover the retaining ring and come to rest as far down on the holder as possible (see specific instructions, page 18).

Tear off the tabs and dispose of them. Now you have a complete unit. Add sterilized water, cover with a nipple and cap, and add the formula when ready for use. Heating will not be necessary. Or pour formula into bottles and store in the refrigerator until needed.

KEEP THE NIPPLES FLOWING

Nipple holes must be the right diameter to let the baby feed easily. If they're not large enough, the baby has to work too hard and therefore may tire of sucking too early and demand another feeding ahead of schedule. If the holes are too large, the formula streams out too fast. The baby may gag or be filled up before the sucking instinct has been satisfied.

To test the nipple, hold the bottle upside down and shake it. The formula should drip fairly rapidly, about one to three drops per second. If it drips in a steady stream, the hole is too large and the nipple should be replaced. If it is slower, you must enlarge the hole. To do this, push a red-hot needle through the nipple from the outside. It's easiest if you insert the blunt end of the needle in a cork, then heat the sharp end with a match or lighter. Enlarge the hole gradually, testing the rate of flow after each insertion until the proper diameter has been reached.

Clean nipples after each use. Butterfat in the milk causes rubber nipples to deteriorate. Wash them in warm, sudsy water, using a small nipple brush. Silicone nipples used with disposable bottles may be turned inside out for easier washing. Be sure to squeeze water through the holes. If formula has caked in the nipples or scum has formed, boil the nipples in water for five minutes to remove it.

TIME FOR A BURP

Both bottle- and breast-fed babies swallow air while feeding. A breast-fed child ordinarily swallows less, because the baby usually sits up to eat, allowing air to escape naturally. But either method may make a child uncomfortable if too much air is swallowed. To relieve the discomfort, the baby must be burped or bubbled.

There are various ways to get rid of the accumulated air. The most popular is to hold the baby upright, with head over your shoulder, which makes for a vertical airway. Pat or rub the back gently until you hear a release of air. Or place the baby, stomach down, on your lap or on a mattress, turning head to the side and supporting it with your hand while you rub the back with the other hand. Another method is to

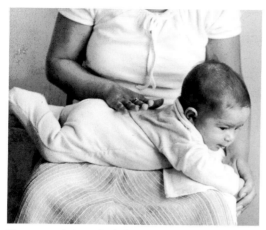

Three ways to burp the baby:
newborns burp best on stomach, in
your lap. Pat or rub the baby's back.

An older baby may be held upright,
with its head nestling against your
shoulder. Pat back gently.

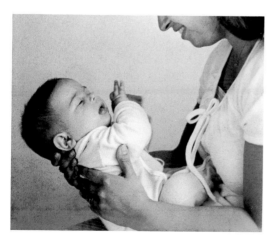

Some babies burp best when placed
in a sitting position. Support head
and back, then pat.

hold the baby in a sitting position, leaning slightly forward, with your hands propping head and back. Often, simply moving the baby into that position will bring up the air.

Two burps during the feeding and one afterward are usually enough, unless the baby still seems distressed. Some nursing mothers automatically burp the baby when they switch breasts. Don't interrupt the feeding to burp the baby. Wait until there's a pause in the nursing.

Although most babies burp two to three times during and after feedings, it's not unusual for babies *not* to burp as expected. Don't worry. Give up your burping efforts after one to two minutes if unsuccessful.

After burping, place the baby in bed on the stomach. That allows for release of any additional air, and if the baby should happen to spit up, milk or mucus won't get into the lungs. If the baby doesn't like the stomach position, place him or her on the side and prop the head with a pillow or blanket.

SPITTING UP

Spitting up during burping or after feeding is common. It isn't significant if the baby is gaining weight. Spitting up after feeding is seldom like the projectile vomiting of illness. Milk just seems to trickle from the mouth and usually contains a few undigested curds.

For unknown reasons, some babies seem to spit up more than others. It may indicate the baby has swallowed too much air during feeding. If spitting up persists, try burping the baby longer. More time in an inclined chair may help, too.

Some babies continue to spit up persistently despite these measures. The explanation then may be not swallowed air but immaturity of the muscles controlling the passage between the esophagus and stomach. This theory is supported by the fact that spitting up gradually lessens as the child grows older.

Vomiting with force should be reported to the doctor, especially if it occurs after several feedings or continues for several days. Repeated vomiting may dehydrate the baby and may indicate illness.

BOWEL MOVEMENTS

The baby's first bowel movements usually are greenish-black. The dark color indicates the presence of meconium, a substance in fetal wastes that continues to appear during the transition to independent life. The odorless, tarry stools last only about three to four days. Afterward, bowel movements may vary according to whether the baby is breast- or bottle-fed.

Breast-fed babies commonly have loose, watery, diarrhea-like stools during the first month. There may be as many as six to nine a day, perhaps one after each feeding. Some may be little more than a stain on the diaper. The looseness is normal and isn't true diarrhea, which is usually signaled by an abrupt change in frequency or consistency of stools.

On the average, breast-fed babies have more frequent, looser bowel movements, but this is by no means an inflexible rule; in both breast- and bottle-fed babies, the consistency and frequency can be highly variable. The range may vary all the way from no movements to nine or ten a day. The stools may be almost completely liquid, or appear as firm pellets. The color is most commonly yellow and pasty, but movements may be brown, orange, green, or black. None of these variations in color, consistency, or frequency—or even a change in these qualities—is cause for alarm if the baby seems well otherwise.

"Diarrhea" and "constipation" can be difficult to define with this much normal variation. In general, "diarrhea" is suspected if there is an abrupt increase in frequency and looseness, especially if there are other signs of illness such as decreased appetite, irritability, and vomit.

Many babies strain heartily, groan, and turn beet-red while having a bowel movement, but this does not represent constipation, especially if the movements are of normal consistency when they do appear. The baby usually is considered constipated if the stools are both hard and difficult to pass. Sometimes such movements may cause cracks around the anus, and flecks of blood may appear in the stool. If hard stools are a problem, offer the baby water between feedings, or ask your doctor for other suggestions. In general, constipation in the adult sense seldom is a problem in young babies.

CHANGING DIAPERS

Change the baby's diapers after every bowel movement and as often as practical after urination. Put on a fresh diaper after a bath and after a feeding. That usually adds up to about 12 changes a day.

A wet diaper isn't an emergency, however. Don't wake the baby to change a diaper; babies wake if they feel uncomfortable. If the baby is warm otherwise, he or she won't be chilled even if a diaper is soaked.

After a bowel movement, wipe the diaper area with soft toilet tissues that can be flushed away afterward. Cleanse the skin with a soft damp cloth or with moistened cotton balls. Pat dry with a soft clean cloth, being sure to dry the creases. It's not necessary to apply powder. Some doctors suggest a hair dryer on a low setting aimed at the diaper area.

To change a diaper, place the baby on his or her back. Unpin the diaper, placing the pins out of the baby's reach. Fold the diaper under as you unpin, and remove. Wash and dry the diaper area. Lift the baby's legs by the ankles and slip a clean diaper under, with the extra thickness in front for a boy, in the rear for a girl. Pin on each side, back overlapping front. Put your finger between diaper and skin to avoid sticking the baby. Keep pins sharp; most pricked fingers are caused by dull pins. Have several sets. Store in soap when not in use.

DIAPER CARE

Whether you launder your own diapers or subscribe to a diaper service, keep a two-gallon covered pail for soiled diapers in the bathroom. A diaper service usually will provide a deodorized pail, along with disposable liners.

After removing a soiled diaper, scrape or shake the stool into the toilet and flush. Rinse the diaper in the clear water until the stain is removed. Wring out and drop the diaper into the pail. Wet diapers may be rinsed under the faucet, wrung out, and placed in the pail.

A diaper service usually will pick up soiled diapers once or twice weekly, along with your baby's other laundry. In some states, the services are licensed and must meet hygiene standards.

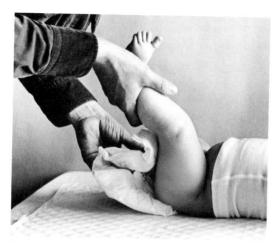

The daily dozen: to change soiled diaper, unpin and place pad under baby to catch moisture.

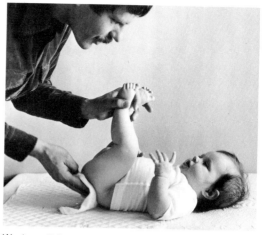

Wash genital area with warm, damp washcloth, including all creases and folds. Pat the area dry.

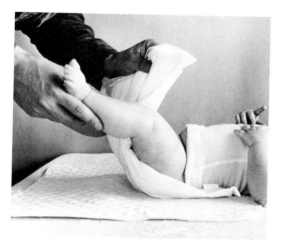

Lift baby by ankles and slide diaper under hips. Bring diaper up between the baby's legs.

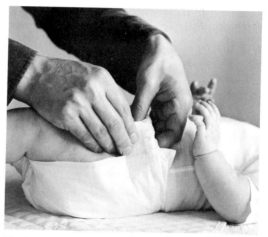

Pin (or tape) diaper on each side. Always keep fingers next to baby to avoid pricking skin.

Laundering diapers in an automatic washer at home adds up to about one-tenth the price of using a diaper service but is less convenient. Adequate rinsing is critical to remove detergent, which can cause skin irritation. If the baby already has a rash, you may need to soak the diapers in a commercial purifying solution, a process described on page 25. Extra rinsing and pre-soaking also help. With proper care, home laundering achieves sterilization.

In laundering flame-retardant sleepwear, avoid powder soaps. Combined with hard water, soaps leave a film that can itself catch fire after several washings. Instead, use phoshate-based detergent, or, where phosphates are prohibited, a heavy-duty liquid.

DISPOSABLE DIAPERS

Diapers you use only once and throw away are even more convenient. And using disposables also cuts down on skin rash, odor, and irritations. They're available at discount stores, supermarkets, and drugstores. Even if you use cloth diapers ordinarily, you'll want a supply of disposables for emergencies and for traveling.

Disposables have three layers—a porous inner layer next to the baby's skin; a waterproof outer covering; and, sandwiched between, several thicknesses of absorbent material. Moisture penetrates the inner layer and is absorbed by the center layer, keeping wetness from the baby's skin. The outer layer substitutes for plastic pants and protects clothing from getting wet. Most disposables are equipped with self-adhesive tapes that replace diaper pins.

DIAPER RASH

Diaper rash isn't a single condition. Instead, the term refers to any skin eruption in the diaper area, where heat and moisture form a natural breeding ground for bacteria. There are several varieties of diaper rash, each of which can make a small baby sore and uncomfortable. All have their own distinctive patterns, which, if recognized, let you treat them quickly and prevent further rashes.

• The most common rash affects the rounded surfaces of the diaper area, such as buttocks and lower abdomen, sparing the folds of skin. It is usually an irritation due to contact with urine. Ammonia formed by the action of bacteria on urine-soaked skin or diaper is considered the major source. Sometimes the rash consists of large red patches, sometimes of rounded, elevated areas of redness and skin breakdown. Most babies have this ammonia-related rash intermittently. It usually responds well to more frequent diaper changes and to letting the baby go without diapers as much as is practical.

• Red, raw places confined to the folds of skin in the diaper area may result from heat and friction, or from the same skin disorder that causes cradle cap. If the rash is caused by heat, remove the baby's plastic pants, because they retain heat and moisture.

• Soreness confined mainly to the rectum and genital area is usually the result of loose stools. Both bottle-fed and breast-fed babies are affected. It may clear without special treatment.

• Sores in the rectal-genital area may result from a yeast infection. These infections tend to cause red patches in the folds of skin, with small red bumps (often with tiny yellow centers) around the periphery. Yeast infections may be treated with an ointment prescribed by your doctor.

• A rash confined to the area of the elastic band in plastic pants at any age is the result of alternate wetting and drying. To prevent it, use diapers, without covering them with plastic pants.

• Tiny blisters and pustules covering the entire diaper area may be heat rash, or prickly heat. The blisters may be found on other parts of the body, too, but are concentrated in the diaper area because of higher temperatures. Fewer clothes will help prevent a recurrence.

• Other rashes, especially those causing large, draining blisters in the diaper area, may indicate more widespread types of skin problems or conditions affecting the entire body. They require a doctor's attention as soon as possible.

To treat all forms of diaper rash, remove diapers as soon as they are wet or soiled. As much as you can, leave the diapers off entirely until the rash heals. To help keep things dry, put two or three layers of diapers and a rubberized pad under the baby in the crib, replacing them as necessary. When you must diaper, use two or three thicknesses of cloth diapers and omit plastic or rubber pants, which may seal in moisture and keep the skin irritated.

In cases of an ammonia-related rash, petroleum jelly or a mild protective ointment may be applied after cleaning and drying, to protect the skin from further contact with urine. Zinc oxide should not be applied while the skin is inflamed but may be used after healing to prevent new inflammation. Avoid powdering with cornstarch, which can be a culture medium for bacteria. If you use baby powder, apply lightly and sparingly, not in large amounts.

An ordinary light bulb, directed toward the exposed area from a few feet away, hastens healing. Cool, wet compresses, soaked in a solution of one teaspoon salt to a pint of water, may be applied intermittently, with "air conditioning" by exposure between applications.

If these simple measures are not successful, a different form of rash may be responsible, or there may be excessive ammonia because diapers have been inadequately sterilized. A strong and persistent smell of ammonia is your first clue. If you launder diapers in an automatic washer at home, several approaches may eliminate ammonia-causing bacteria. Simply adding a cup of chlorine bleach or diaper wash to the laundry may be enough.

Or you can soak the soiled diapers in a commercial diaper-soak product or Borax, then wash with mild laundry detergent, repeating the rinse cycle twice. Acidify the washed and rinsed diapers by adding one cup of vinegar to half a washtub of water, soaking the diapers for about 30 minutes and then spinning dry without further washing.

Finally, the simplest but most expensive course is to use a commercial laundry service.

BATHING THE BABY

A bath is an important part of the routine, but you needn't bathe the baby every day. It's strictly an individual and cultural matter. American babies, for instance, are bathed twice as often as European babies, without any difference in the health of either group.

In a warm climate, you may wish to give a bath daily, even sponging the baby off (without soap) every few hours during hot summer months. In winter, you may cut back to a bath every other day or three times a week, because indoor heat lowers humidity and dries out the baby's skin. Frequent bathing increases chafing and itching. The number of baths also should be reduced if the baby has a skin rash. Too much bathing also bothers the baby's delicate skin.

Set a regular place and time for bathing the baby. A bath after a feeding is a good idea, because the baby is less restless when less hungry. Many parents prefer a morning bath, so the baby is dressed in a clean wardrobe for the day. After the bath, the baby can be tucked into the crib or bassinet for a morning nap. In many families now, evening is bath time and the father is the bather. That allows him socializing time with the baby, comparable to the mother's intimate periods of nursing.

Almost any place that's warm, free from drafts, and a convenient height is good for bathing. The kitchen sink will do if it's large enough, or baby's own plastic tub may be placed on the kitchen counter. There is no special magic about a bath table except to be sure the height is right for you to bathe the baby without stooping.

Keep baby's bath supplies together in a tray or basket so you won't have to search for them at bath time. You won't need special toiletries. Any good, mild unscented soap will do. A castile-based soap meets these requirements. Liquid soaps are good. Some soaps are less drying than others; trial and error will establish your preference.

Some parents like to apply baby oil, creams, lotions, or powder to the baby after bathing, but none of these is really necessary. If you use any of them, do so sparingly. Oil may clog the baby's pores. Shaking on powder lavishly may infiltrate the baby's lungs.

Until the baby's navel and circumcision are healed, give sponge rather than tub baths. (For instructions on sponge bathing, see page 27.) Afterward, the baby can graduate to a portable bathtub.

Test the temperature of the water on the inside of your wrist; it should be comfortably warm, not hot.

Whether you're giving the baby a sponge or tub bath, use your hands or a soft cloth and gentle soap. Some parents like to start with the face and work in a head-to-toe fashion; others leave the face for last, because some babies don't like face-washing and may protest vigorously. In either case, wash the face carefully, trying not to get soap in the eyes.

Cleanse the baby's head about three times a week, and rinse with clear water at other times. Work from front to back, so that shampoo or soap doesn't get into the eyes. Scrub well, using the tips of the fingers and not the fingernails; rinse thoroughly. Clean only the outer areas of the ears, using a soft cloth or moist cotton. Don't use a cotton-tipped stick and don't wash the inside of either the nose or ears.

Some parents wait to trim fingernails until the child is sleeping. It's possible, though, that the baby will wake suddenly, with a jerking movement. Another way is to hold the baby securely on your lap while the child is awake, holding the hand with each finger extended individually. Cut nails straight across with a blunt scissors; a pointed scissors may poke the baby's delicate skin.

Many babies enjoy their baths immediately. They splash and kick and squeal with delight. But others find bathing traumatic, howling with protest as soon as they're wet. It may take eight or ten baths before they adjust to the water.

Introduce these reluctant bathers to the experience gradually. Soap and wash them on a towel outside the tub; then immerse them in the water for rinsing only. Be careful when you pick up the squirming, soapy infant. Use the "football carry" illustrated on page 27, placing your arm under the baby's head and back, the other hand supporting the head.

Words of warning: Never leave any baby unattended in the bathtub, even for a few seconds. A few inches of water can be dangerous to a newborn; when you turn away to reach soap or powder, always keep one hand firmly on the baby. If the telephone or doorbell rings, wrap the dripping baby in a towel, and take him or her with you when you respond. In a real emergency, put the child on the floor, where the baby can neither fall nor drown.

NAVEL AND CIRCUMCISION

The stump of the umbilical cord usually falls off within ten days after birth, although it may remain for four weeks. Meanwhile, the area must be kept clean and dry. Cleanse it at least once daily, washing with a cotton ball soaked in rubbing alcohol, then drying with a clean cotton ball or soft cloth.

After the cord drops off, there may be secretions from the navel, and a spot or two of blood may appear. The spotting may continue for several days. This is normal; continue to clean the area until oozing stops. If bleeding continues more than a week, notify a doctor.

Circumcision requires no bandage or dressing, either. If the circumcision has been performed by encircling the penis with a plastic ring, the ring will drop off within a week or ten days. If the foreskin has been removed by a different method that does not use a ring, apply petroleum jelly to the healing area after each diaper change to prevent sticking.

SWOLLEN BREASTS

Both boys and girls may have swollen breasts at birth—the result of maternal hormones still in the baby's bloodstream. The swelling eventually will disappear. Milk may drain from the breasts, too. It is not necessary to attempt to extract the remainder of this so-called witches' milk. It is harmless and will disappear within a short time after birth.

A few baby girls may have slight, blood-tinged vaginal discharge, also due to the mother's hormones. The condition is normal and requires no special treatment. It usually stops within a few days.

When a baby girl is bathed or her diaper changed, the vulva should be cleaned with moist cotton. Always work from front to back, so fecal matter does not contaminate the vaginal area. Be sure to dry the folds of the vulva well to prevent rash and irritation.

DRESSING THE BABY

With modern central heating, swaddling the baby isn't necessary. Dress the baby in the amount of clothes that makes you comfortable. If you're not wearing long sleeves, the baby also will be hot in clothes reaching the wrists. If you're cold without a sweater, the baby also will require an outer wrap of some sort.

The baby usually wears two layers of clothing. The layer next to the skin consists of a diaper and undershirt. This first layer is covered by a kimono or gown that ties or snaps in front or back, or a one-piece jumpsuit, with full-length sleeves and built-in booties. In the crib, the baby usually will be wrapped in a lightweight cotton receiving blanket. A heavier blanket should not be necessary except when baby goes outdoors.

When the temperature outdoors exceeds 75 degrees Fahrenheit, you usually can remove the receiving blanket. At 80 degrees, the baby doesn't need the jumpsuit or kimono. On a hot summer day, the baby will be comfortable in nothing more than a diaper.

Of course, during cold weather, you'll want to keep the baby out of drafts, even though there is not firm evidence that drafts cause illness.

HOW TO GIVE A SPONGE BATH

Baby's first bath is usually a sponge bath. Tubless cleansing continues for the first three or four weeks, until navel and circumcision are healed. Then the baby is ready for his or her own tub.

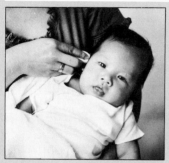

Wash only outer areas of the ears, using soft cloth or cotton. Don't use cotton-tipped stick or swab.

Shampoo scalp three times a week with mild soap. Use fingertips, not fingernails. Rinse well.

Use "football carry": your arm goes under the baby's head and back; your hand holds the head.

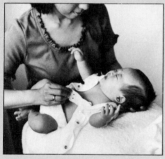

Getting prepared for a sponge bath: sit on low chair and undress baby on towel in your lap. Don't remove diaper.

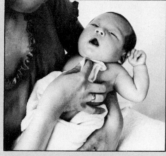

Remove shirt, but keep legs covered. Soap the baby's chest, arms, and hands, including folds and creases in the skin.

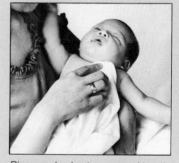

Rinse neck, chest, arms, and hands with clean, warm water. Rinse soap from folds of the skin. Pat the baby dry; don't rub.

Gently, but firmly, support the head, turn the baby on right side to soap, and rinse his or her back and buttocks. Pat dry.

Remove the baby's diaper. Soap and rinse abdomen, genitals, legs, and feet. Wash gently around the navel until the area heals.

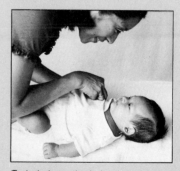

To help keep the baby dry, use powder or cornstarch in the baby's diaper area if you wish. Dress the baby quickly.

HOW TO GIVE A TUB BATH

Bathing a baby isn't a big deal. It may quickly become a highlight of the baby's schedule but needn't be done every day. Three times a week is enough. Have supplies ready before starting.

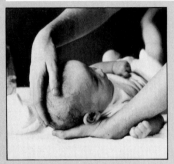

For tub bath, place baby first on soft towel. Wash face with clear water, then shampoo.

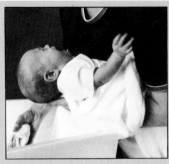

Don't forget football carry (page 27) when rinsing the head. Dry face and hair immediately.

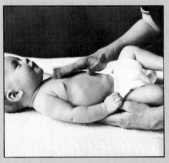

Remove shirt and soap the baby's chest and stomach. Keep the diaper unpinned but in place.

With hand under the baby's armpit, turn the baby over. Then soap back and buttocks. Make sure you have a firm grip.

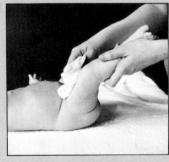

Remove diaper and soap the baby's abdomen, genital area, legs, and feet. Be sure to wash between the baby's toes.

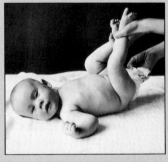

Carefully lift up the baby by the ankles so you can reach and clean all the crevices and creases in the diaper area.

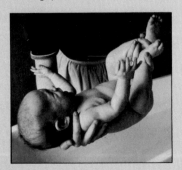

Rinse the baby in clear, warm water. One hand supports the baby's head; the other holds feet and ankles.

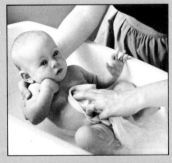

While you keep a firm grasp on the head of the sitting infant, rinse the baby quickly, but thoroughly, with a soft washcloth.

Then, carefully lift the baby out of the tub. Immediately wrap the baby in a large towel, and gently, but thoroughly, pat completely dry.

Dressing the baby is illustrated below. Always dress the baby in clothes that snap or zip their full length so you can change diapers easily. Wrap-around shirts are easier to change than the pullover types. Change the gown or jumpsuit and undershirt if they are wet. You usually can keep the undershirt dry by turning it back at the waist and leaving a gap between the diaper and shirt. All clothes should be loose enough so they can be removed easily and so they allow the baby sufficient freedom to kick and move.

PUTTING THE BABY TO BED

During the first few days of life, babies usually are placed on the side to prevent lying on their healing navels and to reduce the chance of choking on mucus or regurgitated stomach contents. Later many babies prefer sleeping on their stomachs, with heads turned to the side. This helps to release accumulated air and later enables them to raise their heads and look about. However, babies can sleep in almost any position, and some prefer to sleep on their sides or on their backs. All these positions are safe for the baby.

While in bed, the baby should be wrapped in a receiving blanket. A second lightweight blanket may be used but should not be tucked under the mattress. If you lower the heat at night, the baby may need an additional heavier blanket. A blanket made of a synthetic fiber is preferable to one of wool, which may cause a skin rash and is more difficult to launder.

OUT FOR AN AIRING

Babies can be taken outdoors a few days after birth. It's easier in summer, when the baby does not need special clothing. But even a winter baby can go out on a chilly day, provided he or she is dressed appropriately for the weather.

When you dress the baby for an airing, follow the same rules as for indoor wear. To be warm, the baby will need approximately as many layers of clothing as you wear. Indoor wardrobe, a sweater or hooded parka, a lightweight snowsuit or bunting, and a blanket may suffice on cold days. Pick a spot in the sunshine that's well protected from the wind, but be careful about exposing the baby directly to the rays of the sun. Babies get sunburned, too.

At this age, a carriage is best for strolling; if you're just placing the baby on the porch, wheel out the bassinet or portable crib. If you're taking the baby with you while shopping or walking, you may find a canvas baby tote or backpack useful.

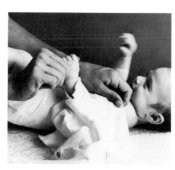

The baby usually wears an undershirt next to the skin. Wrap-around shirts are easier to use than those that pull on over the head.

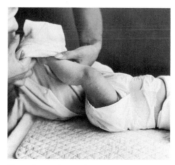

If you're using a jumpsuit, the baby's feet go first. Keep the undershirt dry by turning it back at the waist.

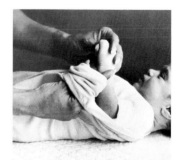

Don't try to place the sleeve over the baby's arm; put your hand inside the sleeve and pull the baby's arm through.

WHEN THE BABY SEEMS ILL

Babies are protected against many childhood illnesses, including measles and mumps if their mothers have had these infections, but they get colds and other viral infections like the rest of us. Strict isolation isn't necessary, but you can protect babies to some degree by discouraging visitors, avoiding obviously ill people, and keeping them from crowded places. A cold is most contagious before any symptoms show. And a baby with older brothers and sisters is likely to be exposed to germs carried home from school.

You don't have to be a doctor to recognize when the baby is ill. A normally cheerful baby who cries continuously, fusses, won't eat, or is listless and lethargic probably is coming down with a cold or other viral infection. Such infections are seldom serious and usually clear up in a few days, but consult the doctor if a child seems ill before age six weeks.

Because the baby can't describe symptoms, a useful clue to illness is the rectal temperature. To measure it, you'll need a rectal thermometer—the type with a large round bulb (see page 31). Shake the thermometer until the mercury reads 96 degrees or less. Then coat the bulb with petroleum jelly. Hold the baby stomach down on your lap or bath table, face turned to one side. Spread the buttocks and insert the lubricated thermometer just beyond the bulb into the rectum. Keep the thermometer in position for two minutes, with the other hand on the baby's back so he or she won't wriggle. Then remove the thermometer and read it. Normal rectal temperatures register higher than the normal oral reading of 98.6°. A rectal reading of more than 100° is considered a fever. After recording the temperature, wipe the thermometer with toilet tissue, wash with warm—not hot—water, and return the thermometer to its case.

It's also possible to take a temperature by holding the thermometer in the baby's armpit. Your pediatrician can show you how this is done. The armpit-axillary method is considered slightly safer since the rectal method may—very rarely— cause an internal injury. A rectal thermometer is used for the axillary technique.

Any fever in an infant under six weeks should be brought to the pediatrician's attention.

But fever alone in an older infant, in the absence of other symptoms, isn't necessarily alarming. A child who remains cheery and playful probably isn't seriously ill, regardless of the temperature. A child who is dull and draggy may need medical attention despite a low or normal temperature.

A fever by itself requires little treatment. Give plenty of fluids, remove extra clothing, and sponge the face and body with cool water. If the fever makes the baby uncomfortable, ask the doctor about medicine to reduce it. Acetaminophen, an aspirin substitute, usually is preferred for children under one year.

Regardless of precautions taken, babies usually have two or three colds their first year— maybe more if they're frequently exposed to other children. Each cold lasts a few days to two weeks. Eyes redden and appetites are lost. Noses run with a clear, watery liquid that later turns thick and sticky. Your baby probably will sniffle a lot, and you can provide relief by sucking out the material with a rubber bulb called a nasal syringe, or aspirator. But no medicine will cure the cold; you and the baby simply have to wait for it to run its course.

VISITING THE DOCTOR

You'll probably return to your obstetrician six weeks after delivery. You'll receive a routine pelvic examination to determine if the uterus and other organs involved in childbirth have returned to normal. The visit will include tests for blood pressure, pulse, and respiratory function; you also may need to give a urine specimen. The doctor probably will check your weight. If you request it, you'll be given contraceptive advice.

Timing of the baby's first post-hospital checkup will vary with the doctor. The doctor may wish to do a checkup two weeks after birth and again at four or six weeks. The main purpose of these early visits with the doctor is for you to ask questions and discuss anything that concerns you. Additionally, of course, the doctor will discuss the baby's feeding and whether he or she is gaining weight satisfactorily, but it is primarily the parents' hour.

WHEN TO CALL THE PEDIATRICIAN

To get the maximum benefit when you call your pediatrician, follow these rules:

• Try to call during office hours, when records are available. Some pediatricians have a period reserved for calls and telephone advice. But don't hesitate to phone after office hours if something troubles you. And call regardless of the hour in the event of emergency, including any of the following: serious accident or injury, bleeding that cannot be stopped, unconsciousness, severe breathing difficulties, convulsions, abdominal pains lasting more than two hours, black or bloody bowel movements, or diarrhea in an infant. If you cannot reach your pediatrician in an emergency, take the baby immediately to a hospital.

• If your child seems sick, always take the temperature before calling the pediatrician.

• The person with firsthand knowledge of the child's condition should speak directly to the pediatrician. Don't relay questions or details through another party.

• Write down pertinent information and questions in advance so you don't forget anything important and have details at your fingertips.

• Have a pencil and paper ready to write down the doctor's instructions.

• Give information on the problem to whoever answers the doctor's phone. Sometimes you don't need to speak to the pediatrician directly. The doctor often can relay the answers to your questions through a nurse or aide.

• Be specific in describing problems or symptoms. Instead of saying, "He has a fever," say, "He has a rectal temperature of 102.6." Instead of reporting that the baby has diarrhea, say, "She has had ten large, watery bowel movements in the last six hours." Be ready to tell the age and approximate weight of the child, how long he or she has been sick, what you think is wrong, and what you have done so far. Pinpoint the location of pains as nearly as you can; describe all symptoms, such as headache or vomiting; and, in case of injury, be ready to describe the accident.

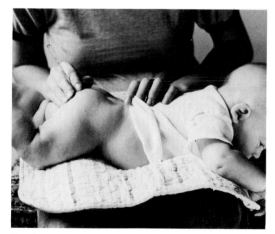

To take a rectal temperature, hold the baby in your lap and immobilize the child with a hand on the back.

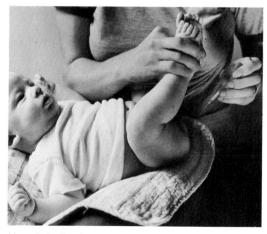

Here, baby lies faceup. Insert the thermometer just beyond bulb; hold in place for two minutes. Temperatures also may be taken at armpit.

WATCH THE BABY GROW

One of the joys of parenthood is watching your child change from a helpless infant into an active, thinking human being. It's like planting a tree and watching it gradually add leaves and branches and reach for the sky.

But babies don't grow like trees, systematically adding a ring each year. Normal children grow in spurts and leaps and at differing rates. They don't even necessarily develop sequentially, the way a tree puts out branches, which then produce other branches. Many children sit before they can stand, but a perfectly healthy minority progresses directly from a horizontal posture to a vertical one and never learns to sit unsupported until the upright stance has been mastered. The usual order for ambulation is to creep, then crawl, then walk. But some children don't creep or crawl at all.

A wiry, active child may pull to a standing position at six months; a heavier, placid one, at 11 months. It doesn't seem to matter. No one has ever shown that a child who walks or talks early grows into a more intelligent, better adjusted, healthier adult.

An activity list that describes when your child may reach certain milestones of development appears on page 37. The timetable is based on the Denver Developmental Screening Test (DDST) calculations of the chronological age at which 50 percent of normal children can perform a given act. This test will be the basis for noting what most normal babies are able to do at a given age.

It is important to note, however, that an equal number can't yet perform the act—and they are just as normal as the others. The median, too, conceals a wide range. Ten percent of normal children take their first independent step before 11 months. But another 10 percent—who also are normal—aren't walking at 15 months.

Similarly, the number of words a child can speak or understand in the last four months of the first year varies widely. Some eight-month-olds repeat sounds that have meaning for them—" Mama" and "Dada," for example, are spoken clearly and applied regularly and consistently to the baby's parents. Other children, equally normal, will not use words in this way until later in the first year.

You'll have fun watching for your baby's firsts and recording them to be remembered later. But remember that a child's development isn't a foot race. If your child crawls earlier or later than the DDST timetable specifies, if he or she can't crawl and the neighbor's child can, indeed even if your child never crawls at all, don't worry about it. Development, to repeat the point, is strictly an individual matter. Watch your baby—not the calendar.

HEIGHT & WEIGHT
BIRTH TO ONE YEAR

Ancestry, not age, often determines a baby's height and weight. A baby with tall parents will probably be tall; one whose parents are slight may have a slim build. These charts illustrate the range of normal growth for children between birth and one year.

Tall — Heavy
Moderately tall — Moderately heavy
Average — Average
Moderately short — Moderately light
Short — Light

BOYS' HEIGHT & WEIGHT   ## GIRLS' HEIGHT & WEIGHT

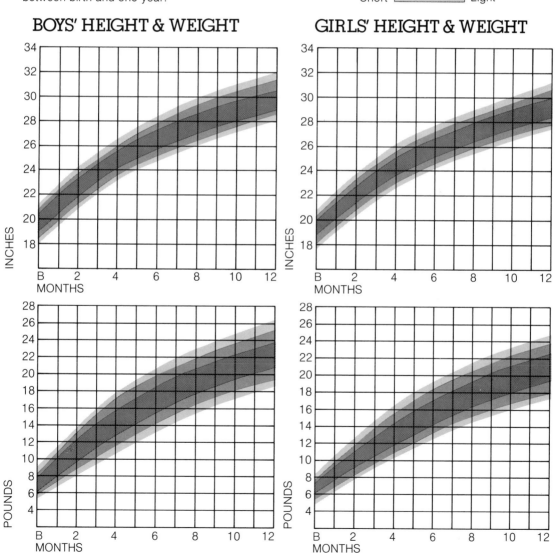

EXERCISES TO BE STARTED AFTER SIX WEEKS

Back builder (below)
Sit on the floor with your right knee bent and your foot flat on the floor. Clasp your hands around the knee. Then using your back muscles, stretch your body toward the ceiling. Be sure to keep your abdomen pulled in and shoulders loose. Repeat this exercise ten times, alternating the knees after each five repetitions.

Trunk tightener (above)
Take position on hands and knees. Swing right arm under left side of body, reaching as far up the back as possible. Turn your head in synchronization with arm. Repeat five times per side. In second exercise (above right), swing arm under body, then raise toward ceiling. Lift head to look at arm. Repeat each five times daily.

Sit-ups (below)
Lie on your back, knees bent, feet flat on floor. Raise your head and shoulders off the floor. Reach forward with hands outside the left knee, then outside the right knee. Repeat three times. In second phase, lift head off floor slowly, then lower gradually. Try to raise your entire back.

Routine exercises begun after six weeks will restore firmness to your midriff and abdomen, if they are performed regularly. It may take six to eight months to get your figure back.

35

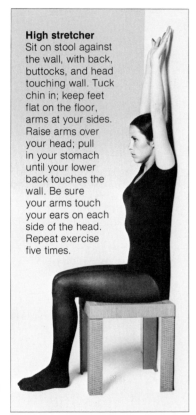

High stretcher
Sit on stool against the wall, with back, buttocks, and head touching wall. Tuck chin in; keep feet flat on the floor, arms at your sides. Raise arms over your head; pull in your stomach until your lower back touches the wall. Be sure your arms touch your ears on each side of the head. Repeat exercise five times.

Touch the chest (above)
To do this exercise, lie on your back with your knees pulled up and hands clasping your bent knees. Pull the knees toward your chest, touching it if possible. Hold this position, then lower your legs very slowly until your feet touch the floor. Now relax and repeat the exercise. Do the exercise six to ten times. Practice it until such time as you are able to touch your chest with your knees on each movement.

Camel walk (right)
Take a "table" position, placing your palms and feet on the floor, feet 12 to 18 inches apart. Keep your knees and elbows straight, and walk around on all fours. Repeat the exercise at least five times daily, moving around the room in this manner once on each attempt. This exercise strengthens the abdominal muscles and helps to reduce the sag that usually occurs in these muscles following delivery.

SIX WEEKS TO THREE MONTHS

HOW THE BABY GROWS

Physically, the average six-week-old probably will weigh ten pounds, having gained three to four pounds since birth and grown to 21½ to 22 inches. The range of size among normal six-week-olds, however, is 7½ to 13½ pounds and 20½ to 24 inches.

The average normal baby, according to the Denver Developmental Screening Test, can achieve the following:
• hold head up at a 45-degree angle when lying on stomach;
• follow an object with eyes for a short distance;
• vocalize with sounds other than crying;
• keep head erect when held in a sitting position;
• smile!

At three months, the average normal baby weighs 13 pounds and measures 24 inches, but normal weight and length may range from 9½ to 16½ pounds and 22 to 25½ inches. Here's what about half of normal babies can do by three months:
• hold head and chest off bed when lying on stomach;
• sit with head steady;
• follow an object moved from one side of head to the other;
• bring hands together in front;
• laugh, squeal, and coo;
• listen to voices and recognize yours;
• smile, socialize, and respond to other people.

THAT FIRST SMILE— AND WHAT IT MEANS

One day during your baby's first two months, you'll gaze into the crib and see a face that suddenly bursts into a bright smile. Maybe the baby will "smile" all over, legs kicking and arms waving like a windmill, wiggling body and head. Your baby—now living up to the legend of a bundle of joy—may even punctuate the smiles with a few gurgles and coos.

That first smile is a marvelous, happy moment for the baby's parents, who until now may have primarily thought of the baby as a hungry mouth to feed and a wet bottom to change. That smile you see and those joyful noises you hear are so spontaneous that at first you may not believe they're genuine.

You'll soon see there's a pattern to the baby's smiles and that they are a definite response to the world, especially to human faces. You'll quickly learn that you can cause a smile by your own behavior. A visit to the crib, a few words, a tickle may cause the baby to grin widely and go into the windmill act.

At first, the smiles that emanate from your baby's crib aren't directed to you. A baby beams at nearly every human face, even a strange or grumpy one. True smiles of recognition don't come until perhaps the fourth month.

Nevertheless, that first smile signals a new and challenging state of development for your fast-changing infant, who now is not only ready for social interaction and stimulation, but needs it as well.

The factors that determine a child's I.Q. are easy to argue about. It *is* known that children who score high on intelligence tests have had (and enjoyed) a great deal of parental stimulation in infancy. Even when they were tiny—too young, seemingly, to understand—their mothers and fathers talked to them, smiled at them, played with them, listened to them, imitated them, responded to them constantly. These babies had many things to look at, listen to, and explore. Even when parents were out of the baby's sight, they chatted, cooed, and sang to the baby. Obviously, these efforts paid off.

Babies are really no different from the rest of us; they too learn from the people around them. Lying helplessly in a crib, a baby offers a smile as an invitation for attention, a way to communicate with you. If that attention is given, the smile is reinforced. The baby smiles again and then moves on to new forms of interaction and learning. If the smile and those that follow are ignored, a baby soon stops smiling—and soon stops reaching out to the world.

YOUR BABY IS AN INDIVIDUAL

A winning smile should remind you that your baby has a unique personality. From the first few days of life, a baby shows a pattern of individuality, just as adults do. You may find that temperament to be quite different from that of an older brother or sister—or the baby next door. No one knows whether these early characteristics are inherited, or develop in the first days of life. It doesn't really matter. The important thing is to recognize that each baby has an individual style. Parenting will be much easier if you observe, recognize, and adapt to these characteristics.

Here are ways normal babies differ and how the differences may affect your care-taking:

Activity Level. Some babies are active; some, quiet. Yours may wriggle constantly while you change a diaper—or just lie peacefully. Both behaviors are normal. A passive baby isn't dull or retarded; an active one isn't bad or reacting negatively to you. But you may need to be extra vigilant in providing safety precautions for a growing, active baby.

Regularity. Some babies seem to have a built-in clock. They demand to be fed at precise four-hour intervals, sleep exactly so many hours, and almost always eat the same amount. Others are wildly unpredictable. Both types develop normally; but for your own peace of mind, you may need to do a little scheduling. Try to feed an irregular baby before the cries come, and put the child to bed on your timetable, not the baby's.

Adaptability. Your baby may reach eagerly for a new toy and love a bath the first time one is given. Or your baby may take a long time to enjoy anything new, kicking and splashing in terror five or six times before a bath becomes pleasant. The baby who resists change requires more patient teaching, but, once adapted, he or she won't be distracted by every new experience.

"Outgoingness." Some babies are shy and withdraw from new faces or new foods, while others immediately respond to novelty. This characteristic differs from adaptability in that it refers to the baby's reaction on first exposure, not how long it takes the child to become accustomed to a situation. Babies who quickly respond to new faces with smiles will delight relatives and visitors. But these babies may be more difficult to keep out of trouble when they're older.

Sensitivity. Some babies seem oblivious to differences in sound, light, taste, or comfort. They can sleep through the loudest noises, the brightest sunlight, the wettest diapers. Others wake at the slightest noise, crying and blinking when lights go on. A child who is very sensitive to disturbances may make life difficult at first. But noticing small differences seems to help the baby learn faster.

Intensity of Reaction. When your child seems pleased, does he or she laugh and wriggle with absolute delight, or just smile quietly? Does your baby merely frown a little when upset—or bellow with rage? If your baby reacts very strongly, you may later have to teach your child that he or she can get what is wanted without resorting to screaming and crying. Fortunately, the child's unbounded delight when he or she is happy compensates for the angry outbursts.

Distractibility. Does your baby stop feeding when another person enters the room? Or does nothing divert the baby's attention? When the baby is crying because of hunger, does a toy provide a momentary distraction, or does the crying continue? You may have to feed an easily distracted baby in a room away from other stimuli. A baby who can't be distracted from an activity, even briefly, requires persistent firmness when you're teaching him or her to change from one thing to another.

Positive or Negative Mood. Some babies are cheerful more than they are fussy or unpleasant. Any baby has good and bad moods, but, on balance, some babies seem to be in a happier frame of mind quite often, while others cry and fuss more frequently.

A baby's difficult moods certainly aren't easy to live with. But moodiness doesn't mean that your methods of child care are wrong. As parents, you must learn to accept some crying and complaining once you've established that the baby doesn't really need anything—food, dry diapers, etc. Chronic negativism can wear you out, though, and you'll need more time away from the child who seems to have more bad than good days.

Attention Span and Persistence. How long will your baby continue trying to do something—even if it is frustrating or if you try to stop the attempt? Will your baby rivet his or her attention on something near the crib for long periods, or turn elsewhere within a few minutes?

True persistence is neither good nor bad. When a baby persists in activities you like or find entertaining or amusing, you'll be pleased; in activities you don't like, displeased. You'll have to be especially firm and patient in distracting a persistent child, steady and encouraging to a less persistent one.

Some babies acquire these traits in combinations that add up to a difficult or confounding personality. It takes a patient parent to deal with the so-called difficult child, for the task is strictly uphill. You need more help from other members of the family. You must be firm time after time when it might seem easier to give in, and you must learn to continue to be approving and affectionate when the child is cooperative.

Difficult babies, fortunately, can learn to be less difficult, and your devotion to this learning process may prevent trouble for the child later on. Although temperamental differences appear within the first few months of life, they are not unalterably fixed; your actions can modify them. In any case, it's important not to label the baby with a trait ("difficult," "easygoing") that may mark and follow him or her throughout life.

It's best to recognize that these traits arise from within the child, and are not a reaction to "good" or "bad" parenting.

The arrival of a newborn will affect the behavior of your other children. Because the baby now has top billing, jealousy is a natural reaction. Assure the older children of your love, but never leave a baby alone with a child under three.

THE SCHEDULE CHANGES

By six weeks, the baby may eat less frequently, giving up one feeding or nursing a day, and stay awake for longer periods. By three months, babies usually are down to four daily feedings—three during the day and one at night. Capacity increases, although the total varies from baby to baby. Now the usual daily amount is about a quart of breast milk or formula, about 32 ounces, every 24 hours.

In addition, the three-month-old baby will let you know in short order when bigger servings are called for. Breast-feeding mothers get the message quickly, because either the baby spends more time at the breast or goes at it more eagerly. The bottle-fed baby announces an increased appetite by gulping two or three consecutive bottles down to the very last drop, then crying or gnawing his or her hands afterward and seeming to look for more.

Some parents fear that feeding the baby as much and as often as he or she demands may condition the child to poor eating habits and cause him or her to grow up obese. But there is no scientific support for this fear.

The baby may lie awake a total of eight hours a day, ready to play and socialize. By six weeks, sleep may come in one long stretch of seven to eight hours—fortunate is the parent when it falls between late evening and early morning—and two to four shorter stretches during the day. Some of these rest periods will be only catnaps, but others may last as long as three or four hours.

By three months, the periods of sleep are usually down to three a day, the pattern your baby will follow through most of the first year. After the last feeding of the evening, the baby now may sleep for ten consecutive hours and then take morning and afternoon naps of about two hours each.

SLEEPING POSITIONS

Between six weeks and three months, depending on size and activity, the baby who has been sleeping in a bassinet should be transferred to a crib. And if the baby has been sleeping in the same room with you, now is the time to provide separate sleeping quarters. Newfound and developing senses now enable even a sleeping baby to detect when parents are nearby, and the baby's restlessness and attempts to attract parents' attention may keep everyone awake.

By now, your baby probably is demonstrating that he or she prefers one sleeping position to another. Usually babies like lying on their stomachs best, and many babies will even protest fussily and refuse to settle down if they are placed in some other position. Some babies seem unable to sleep until they can press their heads into a corner of the crib or against the top of the crib—some authorities believe that perhaps this position is an imitation of the secure position of the head in the womb.

Even awake, many babies may show a preference for one side of the body over the other. For instance, they may always place the right side of their faces against the mattress when looking out through the crib bars or hold their heads to the right when propped in a sitting position. A few babies carry the favoritism to one side of the body or another so far as to favor nursing at one breast in preference to the other. Sometimes these babies actually turn away or fuss if shifted from one breast to another (although some doctors say the difference may be in the breast, not the baby).

No matter what you've heard, allowing the baby to sleep in one position or another won't cause legs or feet to develop improperly. But constantly lying on one side may cause the baby's head to seem flat and lopsided on that side. However much that may alarm you, it won't last long. The head will round out with age, and, in any case, the pressure will be relieved when the child begins to spend more time sitting.

However, if the seeming reshaping of your child's head bothers you and if you want to do something about it, reverse the baby's crib so that he or she must look the opposite way to see into the room. Or you might try to distract the child this way: Hang an attractive toy in a new direction. Another method is to tilt the mattress by placing towels or a blanket under one side, thus compelling the baby to turn the way you prefer.

IMMUNIZATION RECORD			
Child's Name _____ Date of Birth_____			
Immunization	Date	Dose	Physician
DPT	_____	_____	_____
	_____	_____	_____
	_____	_____	_____
	_____	_____	_____
DT booster	_____	_____	_____
Tetanus booster . . .	_____	_____	_____
Polio	_____	_____	_____
	_____	_____	_____
	_____	_____	_____
	_____	_____	_____
	_____	_____	_____
Measles	_____	_____	_____
Rubella	_____	_____	_____
Mumps	_____	_____	_____
Tuberculin test	_____	_____	_____
Others	_____	_____	_____

TIME FOR THE BABY'S SHOTS

At two months, your baby is ready for a first set of immunizations. These usually take the form of a triple antigen, or DPT shot, providing combined protection against diphtheria, pertussis (whooping cough), and tetanus (lockjaw), and a first dose of polio vaccine, given by mouth. Additional DPT shots are recommended at four and six months; a second dose of polio vaccine is given at four months. Boosters of both are recommended at 18 months and at four to six years.

Many babies have reactions to these shots, especially to the pertussis component of the DPT combination. About half of infants may have redness, swelling, or pain at the injection site; about half also have fever and fretfulness. Some infants sleep more than usual. In rare cases there may be convulsions, and in exceedingly rare cases, lasting brain damage. It is not clear whether such cases are caused by the vaccine or occurred coincidentally.

It *is* clear, however, that in countries in which the immunization rate declined, such as Great Britain in the late 1970s, the rate of pertussis infection increased dramatically and was associated with many deaths of infants under one year. The American Academy of Pediatrics thus continues to recommend routine immunization as scheduled, although sometimes the pertussis vaccine is given separately or withheld, or boosters may be postponed, especially if the child or another member of the family has had a history of convulsions. The AAP notes that no immunization is totally without hazard, but that in the case of pertussis the benefits continue to outweigh the very small risks.

In the event of fever or other mild shot reaction, the pediatrician may suggest that you give liquid acetaminophen, an aspirin substitute, combined with water or formula. The fever seldom lasts more than a few hours; the pediatrician should be notified if it persists more than 24 hours. Immunizations should be post-poned if the baby seems ill when they are due.

Although some former scourges of children have disappeared (smallpox vaccination, for instance, is no longer required) and others are far less common than in the past, immunizations remain important. Tetanus is a particular hazard in young children and protection against it remains necessary. Any injury or animal bite in which the skin has been lacerated, punctured, or torn may introduce tetanus germs into the wound. Tetanus shots should always be kept up-to-date.

Because of their possible complications and long-range effects, measles and mumps can be serious diseases in young children. Breast-fed babies obtain prolonged immunity to them from their mothers, but this protection usually has declined by the time they are a year old. Some parents unwisely postpone these immunizations until school age because the shots may make the child uncomfortable. Although measles, in particular, has dwindled to a handful of cases, shots are still recommended early in the second year of life, because the child may be exposed to germs by other young children.

Rubella (German measles) is a minor disease even in small children. Immunization is given mainly to protect the mother and other women of childbearing age with whom the baby may come in contact.

Vaccines against chickenpox and certain bacterial causes of meningitis and pneumonia are being tested. Ask your pediatrician if they are now available for general use. The following general immunization schedule is recommended by the American Academy of Pediatrics:
• two months—DPT, oral polio vaccine;
• four months—DPT, oral polio vaccine;
• six months—DPT (oral polio vaccine optional);
• 12 months—tuberculin test;
• 15 months—measles, mumps, rubella (given as one shot);
• 18 months—DPT, polio boosters;
• 4 to 6 years—DPT, polio boosters.

YOUR OWN
SHOTS RECORD

Keep a personal record of the baby's immunizations, and have the doctor or nurse enter each shot as it is administered, along with the date. That way, you'll know when the last shots were given and when others are due, without waiting to be reminded by the doctor's office.

Also, if you change doctors or move to another community, it'll be convenient to have your own listing of shots. In the event of injury, the record can be particularly important to determine the most recent tetanus inoculation.

Most states now require that your child have a complete record of immunizations before he or she can be admitted to school—another reason to have a record that is accessible. Your immunization record should look like an enlarged version of the one on page 42.

SITTING UP
AND GOING OUT

Now that your baby has become more social, he or she will want to spend more time in sight of you and the rest of the family. An inclined infant seat will enable the baby to sit up and see you. Don't, under any circumstances, prop or place a baby alone and unsecured on a sofa or chair.

Pick a sturdy infant seat. It should be of molded fiberglass, slanted so the baby is held in a semisitting position by the force of gravity from which he or she can't pitch forward. It should have a secure strap and sides high enough to prevent slipping to the side, and it should be supported at the rear so it cannot tip over backward.

The best place for the infant seat is on the floor. That way, an active baby won't topple far if his or her gyrations do tip the chair over (and they no doubt will). Always be sure the restraining strap is snugly fastened, but not tight.

Another way many parents keep a small baby close to them is by using a baby tote or backpack. They've been used for centuries to transport babies while parents keep their hands and arms free to work. The baby rides in a canvas or plastic sling strapped over your shoulders and rests on your chest or back. You can talk to and nuzzle the baby while you go about your household or other duties.

A stroller may well be the baby's first set of wheels. Lightweight, collapsible models are best. They should have a wide wheelbase and large double-front wheels that turn easily.

A baby who holds his or her head up with little effort also may be ready for a stroller. One of the best investments in baby equipment is a lightweight aluminum, collapsible model. The baby rests in a sling, in a semisitting position, and is secured firmly across the middle.

Buy a stroller that can be opened with one hand and folds compactly. Strollers with turnable—instead of fixed—front wheels are easier to maneuver, especially when you're steering with one hand. When driving with the baby, pack the stroller in the car until you reach your destination.

As for the baby's car seat, if you did not purchase one to transport your newborn home from the hospital, you should do so now.

Under federal standards that took effect on January 1, 1981, all seats manufactured after that date must meet dynamic crash-test standards. They will all hold a child securely in a 30-mph crash and even keep him or her in position in a rollover accident. Child seats must now be marked with the date of manufacture and with the words "dynamically crash tested." Some seats made before 1981 (which you may have inherited or found in a garage sale) give good crash protection but do not necessarily meet current government standards.

The safest model for an infant is a rearward-facing seat resembling an inclined baby rest. The baby rides in a semi-upright position, secured with a harness and surrounded by impact-absorbing materials. A parent alone in the car may install the infant seat in the front passenger seat; otherwise the child is always safest in the rear seat.

You can buy an infant seat that will provide protection until the child is about nine to 12 months old (about 17–20 pounds); or a slightly more expensive convertible model, which is designed to face rearward for an infant, then can be reversed to face forward until the child is about four years old, or weighs about 40 pounds. Although more costly at first, a convertible seat is a better buy in the long run.

Booster seats are used after the child outgrows an infant seat, if you have not purchased a convertible model. They are designed for children from 20 to 65 pounds. Most are used in combination with the car's shoulder-lap belt.

Another type of seat surrounds a slightly older child with a protective fiberglass shield that

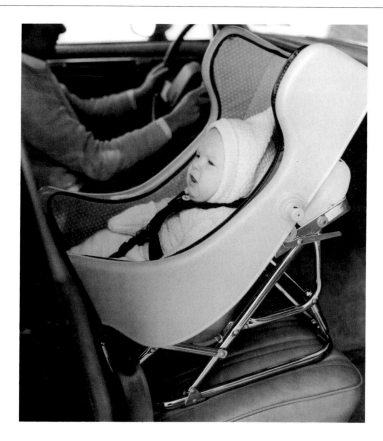

Baby's first car seat faces to the rear and should be mounted in the front passenger seat when only the driver is present. The seat can be moved to the rear when older passengers are in the car. The seat should be labeled "dynamically tested," meaning the baby is protected in event of a crash.

requires no harness. The padded shield acts as a cushion in the event of a crash. A lap belt circles the shield and holds it in place. However, an active child may climb out of the seat while you are driving.

Some seats for toddlers and preschoolers (and convertible models made before January 1, 1981) require a top anchor strap to meet crash standards. This strap must be fastened to a special anchor plate installed to the rear or clipped to the rear seat lap belts, and must always be pulled tight. Properly used, it provides an extra margin of protection, but may require extra effort and expense to install, especially in hatchbacks and station wagons.

Whichever seat you choose, use it on every auto trip, no matter how short. And use your own seat belt, as an example of the need to buckle up.

ON LONGER TRIPS

Tiny babies usually are ideal traveling companions because they're light, portable, and very adaptable. They sleep a lot, don't get restless, and are easy to carry. Travel with infants is far easier than in the past because you can buy bibs, bottles, diapers, and towels that can be thrown away as they're used—even disposable plastic bags to contain the refuse.

In an automobile, the very young baby should travel in a safety seat, just as on shorter trips. The semi-upright position is all right for naps, too. A slightly older baby can occupy a baby rest or seat restraint. No child should travel unrestrained in a moving car. In some states, transporting a child under four without a restraint is a ticketable offense; older children must wear seat belts.

If you notify the airline in advance (at the time you make reservations, say), you usually can reserve the bulkhead seat with a bassinet that attaches to the wall in front of you. Flight crews on most airlines usually will warm formula for you, and some airlines even provide an emergency supply of disposable diapers.

Bring your collapsible stroller, which will be a godsend for transporting the baby around airports, especially when you have other articles to carry. Most airlines will let you include it in your carry-on luggage. A flight attendant will stow it in the closet as you board.

CRADLE CAP

During the first few weeks, a scaly crust may form in the center of the baby's scalp. So-called cradle cap results from overactivity of the oil glands and resembles adult dandruff. The oil glands are stimulated by the hormone testosterone. The overproduction of testosterone is another by-product of the hormones present in the mother's placenta.

The condition isn't a serious one, although cradle cap can be unsightly. Mild cases can be controlled by washing with a soft cloth and mild soap. In more stubborn cases, rub a small amount of mineral or baby oil into the scalp to loosen the flakes. Rub the oil in well. Allow it to soak, then wash the baby's head with mild soap and a washcloth. Then comb and brush the scalp as thoroughly as possible, making sure to use a brush with medium bristles, until all loose flakes of cradle cap are removed completely. For severe cases or if the child has thick hair, you may have to use a tar or anti-dandruff shampoo.

Cradle cap often persists because parents are afraid to massage or rub the soft spot in the baby's skull. Actually, even vigorous massage with the fingertips won't hurt the baby and is essential to remove all the scales. Usually one or two treatments are all that's necessary, but repeat the treatment if the cradle cap recurs.

TIME FOR PLAY

Babies play almost from birth. Many people are not aware of it, because it's not the organized, purposeful activity an adult considers play. At this point, though, babies begin to play with their hands. The experience of discovering those hands can be as much fun for the observer as it obviously is for the baby. Watch as they hold one hand in front of them, perhaps for minutes on end, bring it to their mouths experimentally, or inspect toys held in their hands. They'll hold up both hands, shift their gaze from one to the other, and move them toward each other, watching the light and shadow. Gradually—often after several unsuccessful tries—they will bring them together until they meet and lock, then squeal with delight.

Your baby's eyes can now focus clearly and follow movement, as the hand play indicates.

The baby may gaze for many minutes at a picture on a nearby wall, or at an attractive toy just out of reach, or at your face. He or she may watch as you walk back and forth through the room and follow your shadow as it falls across the bed.

The baby is now ready for toys. Lucky for most parents there's no need to buy expensive toys—because, as the hand exploration shows, enjoyment comes from something as simple as watching fingers move.

You don't need to fill the crib with costly stuffed animals or furry creatures. Instead, suspend a mobile over the crib, where it can be seen as it moves when the bed moves. Soft, lightweight toys, especially if they're easy to grasp, also can be part of the learning process.

SITTERS AND CHILD CARE

How soon you leave the baby for an evening out or a visit to friends is strictly up to you. There's no reason not to leave an infant in the care of a baby-sitter right from birth, if you feel well enough and are secure about it. A baby under three months of age won't notice the difference. But be sure to choose your sitter carefully. Even a relative, friend, or neighbor can be less than fully reliable or responsible. A reliable baby-sitter can only make your evening out more enjoyable.

Even at three months, it's best that the baby be awake when the sitter arrives, so the two of you can be seen together. Invite the sitter to come before your departure to see how you hold, handle, and care for the baby. Even young babies like to be treated in a way that's familiar to them. Show your baby-sitter where things he or she will need are kept, and observe closely as she or he feeds and diapers the baby, so you are sure the sitter knows and cares about the baby.

There are no hard-and-fast rules about when a new mother should return to a full-time or part-time job, and often the question is decided by economics or career commitment. Some specialists in child behavior say there is no substitute for the natural parent in the first two years of an infant's life, although others maintain that a well-loved child can thrive in the care of

> **Any time you leave your baby, no matter how briefly, make sure the sitter has the following information:**
> - where you can be reached;
> - telephone numbers of the doctor, hospital and emergency room, fire department, and police (keep them posted next to the phone);
> - the name and telephone number of a responsible friend, relative, or neighbor who can be called if you can't be reached;
> - details about your house—how to regulate heat, how to lock and open the doors;
> - what and when to feed the baby;
> - when you will return;
> - what exactly you expect from the sitter while you're gone.

another if the parents compensate for their absence during periods of reunion. You may want to limit the time you and the child are separated, and strike some balance between your need to work and the child's emotional needs.

In any case, the decision is not one to be made offhandedly, but should be planned carefully and agreed to by both parents, even before childbirth. Once reached, however, it is not a decision to feel guilty about.

Unless the father can take over the domestic role, the mother's return to work requires some kind of professional, full-time baby care, either in your own home, in another's home, or in a day-care center. No professional baby care is inexpensive, and all require careful thought before the choice is made. The matter of leaving your child in the care of another is worrisome, too. Ask friends for their recommendations, and explore all possibilities before you choose.

The best and least expensive full-time baby-sitters often are trusted friends or relatives. You usually know them well enough to have faith in their reliability and responsibility, you know they will have an interest in your child, and you can expect them to care for the baby the way you would do it yourself. Hiring a sitter or house-keeper and training him or her to care for the baby is a more expensive and difficult proposition. You may have to spend long hours teaching and supervising the person (however, the effort is certainly worth it). If you have several children, though, a sitter who can come to your house while you're away is often the best solution.

For a young child, care within a private home often works most satisfactorily. That's because the rhythm of home life is nearer to the child's own experience. Too, your child should get more attention because smaller numbers of children are involved.

Some state agencies license private homes where children are cared and inspect them for safety. Unfortunately, most states have no licensing for personnel.

Commercial day-care centers and those operated by nonprofit or charitable agencies are proliferating. Properly staffed and supervised, they may provide the best care, especially for children above the age of three. They also can be the most economical.

Before choosing a day-care home or center, you'll want to visit and examine it. Have these questions answered:

- Are you welcome to visit the day-care center at any time, and are your suggestions for care of your child welcomed and put to practice? (And if not, are you told why?)
- Does the person or persons caring for the children seem to really care about them, or are those persons impersonal with them?
- Is the home or center clean, safe, airy, and healthful-appearing, with sufficient space for the children to play?
- Is there at least one adult for every four or five older children (or two or three infants), including the person's own children?
- Do the staff and the children seem to be happy and enjoying themselves?

If you find something you don't like about the way your child is cared for, don't hesitate to speak up and demand change. If you are not satisfied, be prepared to make other arrangements. The most important aspect of child care is your confidence that your child is in good hands.

INDEX